T0322108

Find Your Own Path

Find Your Own Path

How to Create the Life You Really Want

FIONA BUCKLAND

MICHAEL  JOSEPH

PENGUIN MICHAEL JOSEPH

UK | USA | Canada | Ireland | Australia
India | New Zealand | South Africa

Penguin Michael Joseph is part of the Penguin Random House group of companies
whose addresses can be found at global.penguinrandomhouse.com

First published 2023
001

Set in 12.5/14.75pt Garamond MT Std
Typeset by Jouve (UK), Milton Keynes
Printed and bound in Great Britain by Clays Ltd, Elcograf S.p.A.

The authorized representative in the EEA is Penguin Random House Ireland,
Morrison Chambers, 32 Nassau Street, Dublin D02 YH68

A CIP catalogue record for this book is available from the British Library

HARDBACK ISBN: 978–0–241–58729–4
TRADE PAPERBACK ISBN: 978–0–241–58730–0

www.greenpenguin.co.uk

MIX
Paper from
responsible sources
FSC® C018179

Penguin Random House is committed to a
sustainable future for our business, our readers
and our planet. This book is made from Forest
Stewardship Council® certified paper.

To my family

Contents

Preface

The first panic attack came for me when I was forty-two. It had been stalking me undetected for a while, waiting for the perfect moment for the inevitable meeting. The road had been smoothed in the preceding years by a series of events that shook my foundations: a relationship ended, my brother suffered a critical illness, I experienced a severe episode of depression and left what I had believed would be my secure job and home. I unconsciously tried to plug the chasm that opened up below me with my fail-safe habits of work, socializing and taking care of others. But now, although I was pulling the old levers, the machinery wasn't responding. My life had run out of road and I needed to find another way forward.

I was born the only child of an unmarried Irish nurse, who died of breast cancer when I was two years old. I was eventually adopted by my English foster parents. They rarely talked about my birth mother and I grew up not wanting to upset them by asking. I spent a lot of time alone, reading, playing in the garden or dancing in my room. I was bright but bored, and often in trouble at school. All I had of my birth mother was a photograph of me as a toddler sitting on her knee on our last Christmas together. If I could show you this picture now, you would see some gifts scattered around, with a white tinsel Christmas tree in the background and the kind of seventies furniture that's become achingly fashionable again. She is gazing down at little me, so when I look at the photo, I can't see her face. I can't consciously remember her now, and many times over the years I held the picture flat in my palm, tilting it this way and that, as if by some miracle her chin would lift and I could see her again. But she remained out of reach.

I left home without a goal, but with curiosity and a love of learning about the world and the stories of people in it, which drew me to the path of academia. Eventually I did a PhD in Performance Studies at New York University. I still loved to dance and sensed that there was something important being created when people danced together in social spaces. I made this the focus of my research and interviewed people who went to lesbian and gay clubs, who told me that they performed the stories of their true selves and created community when they danced.

My PhD complete and first book published, I returned to the UK with an instinct that my next big adventure lay not in the slow lane of academia but in the new frontiers of e-commerce. I joined the team at a big online book retailer – an evangelizing upstart at the time. We knocked on the doors of publishers and cockily informed them that we were the future. After a few years, one of them poached me. So it was that I found myself approaching forty with a corporate career, a long-term relationship, a mortgage and a growing realization that this could be what my life would look like for the next twenty-five years. I was coasting. I rarely danced any more. Then came the series of life events that shook all this apart.

I managed and coped – for a while at least. Then one morning, I awoke breathless, heart racing. Unable to stand, I slid out of bed and landed in a heap on the floor. Something had finally caught up with me. Now I had to understand what.

A good friend saw my distress and suggested therapy. It was a leap of faith. The process couldn't promise to make me better, but it could make me different – if I chose to be. Yet I held fast to a story of loss and abandonment through which I framed my life experience. I couldn't conceive of any other possible story because of a terrible, unspoken belief which unconsciously ran my life: I was the cause of my mother's death. I believed that my birth had triggered her cancer. Out of loyalty to her and in fear of a dreadful reckoning, I had lived my life up to that point unconsciously convinced that I would die at the same age as her. I couldn't imagine living for a moment longer than she had. As I approached that birthday, the panic attacks were internal alarm bells ringing to attract my attention. 'Here!' they hollered. 'Something deep in you needs to speak, and you need to listen. Your old life has come to an end; you must imagine a new one so you can live.'

My old story felt like a coat I had worn for so long I had forgotten it wasn't my skin. I had to free myself from my tenacious old narrative of loss, my vicious inner critics and saboteurs, and my habitual achieving, working and partying to cope, so that I could create a new, more authentic and meaningful story, forged by who I was at heart. My mother was dead at forty-six, but I wasn't. I had to *believe* I could live a different life, then *choose* to live it. It was as if I had been living in a big house with many rooms but had chosen to stay in the kitchen where I felt comfortable. But someone kept knocking on the front door and the pipes clanked in distant, boarded-up rooms. I kept turning up the music to block them out, but they became louder and louder, until they eventually threatened to shake the edifice apart. So I opened the door, to find a part of myself standing there asking, 'Why don't you let me speak? Why won't you care for me?' I brought that deeper part of me inside, and we started to open my house together, room by room. There was so much more to me than I could have imagined or lived up to that point, and although the process felt painful at times, it was less so than living a smaller life, disconnected from who I was at heart.

This was the start of my inner work. It wasn't until I had opened out more of those rooms that I could begin to figure out who I could be in the world from the inside out. I needed to know and accept myself more before I could forge an authentic path for myself.

Outer changes didn't happen immediately, which is important for you to know. Sometimes I still say, 'Hey, universe, I want my cup filled with exactly what I want, in exactly this measure, and I want it now, please.' If you can relate to this impatience, there's no shame. I have discovered that being so focused on the cup, I can miss everything around me waiting for me to notice it.

Sometimes the signs are there, but it takes a while to see them. It took redundancies from three jobs that, in retrospect, I was not entirely comfortable in before I finally got the message that sitting in the corporate or managerial chair might not be where I could feel most authentic, fulfilled and impactful, no matter how amazing the chair. In my personal life, relationships didn't end up in ways that perhaps I hoped for, although I made some lifelong friends. I had to move home again and again – sometimes pulled, sometimes pushed. Sometimes the path opens up in front of you. Sometimes it is shaped by the paths that close behind you. At a certain point – the one you have arrived at – I decided to put my hands on the wheel of my life rather than react to events or hold on to old, false beliefs and ways I had done things in the past. I set out to discover what would fulfil me now, and actively find my own path. It's an illusion to imagine that we have complete control over our lives, but if we can check that our ship is sound, our shipmates on board and our hands on the wheel, then we can steer through storms a little more easily, adapt more thoughtfully and hold true to our North Star, even if we get blown off course sometimes.

At the beginning, I felt a bit lost and didn't know how to start. What made all the difference was working with a life coach. With his help, I took another leap of faith to explore the question that was now important to me: how can I bring my essential nature, potential, experience and passions to be of service in the world? The steps I took led me to my career as a coach, facilitator and writer, helping others explore the same question that continues to mean so much to me. But this wasn't only about my career. In my personal life, I am more loving, honest, vulnerable and compassionate with myself and others, and I have much better boundaries. I discovered that so much of what I already was had laid the foundations upon which I could build, and I could also develop and learn more. You'll probably discover that too. You are not starting from scratch, and you are not finished yet.

My life story has given me many resources. I care about my own and others' growth, love learning and creating, and can lean as deeply into others' feelings as I am able to with my own. I can accept my own messiness more, and can accept my clients' wholeheartedly. I believe in taking action, and in being a positive influence in the world – professionally and personally – because the world needs us. Now I bring all of this to coach people to find their own paths, on which, rather than following the internal and external scripts that run their lives, they connect with their authentic selves and become the authors and creators of more meaningful lives. I also work with people who want to take leadership not only of their own lives but of people, projects and organizations, making the world a better place in the process. I believe that we are all leaders, whether we see ourselves that way or not, and when we find our own path, we give permission to others to do the same.

Today, I fold more of who I am into my work and life, and help others to do likewise. I feel great joy at the privilege of life itself, a gift given to me by my mother. I have crossed over a threshold into a life I could never have imagined would be my own – in which I can choose to live more fully.

Until recently, however, there was one place I couldn't go. It's a patch of earth in south-west Ireland where my birth mother is buried. For years, I tried to find its location, but my efforts were in vain, and frustratingly, like her face in the photo, she remained hidden. I papered over the door of that room by pretending I didn't care. When I finally allowed my heart to long for it, and stood in front of that door, I had no idea how to open it. Then something extraordinary and wonderful happened. Out of the blue, I received a message via social media from my birth family, whom I had never considered contacting in case they didn't know or want to know about me. I received more than one gift that day. I discovered that the world was bigger than I had imagined and included magic, mystery and blessings outside of my logical understanding. Only when I asked for what I truly wanted could I receive what I had never imagined possible.

When I travelled to Ireland a few months later, I discovered my birth family had kept a treasure trove of photographs. Finally, I could see the faces of both my parents, so full of life and love. The family had even held on to my christening robe as a talisman, hoping one day I would find them and they could return it to me. I held the white lace in my hands, struck by the smallness of the collar through which my baby neck had once slipped. With astonishment, I understood how tiny I had once been, how vulnerable, how utterly dependent on the love of my mother, and how loveable. Now it was time. My relatives pointed me towards the place where my mother lies buried and left me to go there alone.

By the ruins of the old chapel, under grey skies, I sat on the grass next to her grave, and the words came simply: 'Hello, I found you again.' As I uttered them, the sun came out and touched my face with warmth, and it felt like her love. In that moment, I realized that I had rewritten my story from one of loss to one of love. Although I hadn't been able to see her, she had seen me, caught in that moment by the photographer, gazing at me, loving me.

We are at a point when people are looking at the work they do, where they live, who they live with and the lives they lead, and saying, 'Enough.' Whatever brought them to seek out my coaching services, without exception each of my clients wants to find their own path, rather than stay stuck in jobs, relationships, locations and lives that ask much while simultaneously reducing their sense of authenticity and meaning. You are standing on the threshold of an old life you have outgrown or left, peering through to see if you can discern what might become your path. I am sending you a signal from the other side: you have the power to write your own story. This is what you are feeling the call to do. Whatever has brought you here, you are now ready to put your own hands on the wheel of your life and – rather than reacting to external events and the inner storms which can blow us off course – steer it in alignment with who you are at heart.

It takes inner work to make outer change, and this is what I am going to help you to do, by giving you some tools. What you'll learn you'll put into action, and it will transform your life in ways you might not yet be able to imagine right now, so take a small leap of faith. I know not everyone can have a life coach of their own, which is why I have written this book. I have helped others and I hope this book will help you. I stand with you on the edge of something big. I am excited for you, however lost you might feel right now. When I work with a new client, it's as if I am opening a new book, with an as yet unknown journey ahead. You have opened your book. This is your time to write the next chapter of your story. Let's begin.

Introduction

Midway upon the journey of our life
I found myself within a forest dark,
For the straightforward pathway had been lost.
Dante Alighieri, *The Divine Comedy:*
Inferno, Canto I, translated by
Henry Wadsworth Longfellow

If you are living your life right, there may come a time
when you find yourself – like Dante – lost. What once
brought you joy now feels flat and small. You might
have that Sunday evening dread of returning to work
that once excited you but now feels heavy and chore-like.
You might look at the people with whom you spend most
time, where you live, what you talk about, and how you
spend the precious hours and days of your life and feel
strangely uninvolved, drained, restless or frustrated. You
repeat the strategies that quietened discontent in the past,
only to find they no longer work. Then there are events
such as a pandemic, redundancy, the failure of a project
or business, bereavement, illness, retirement, relationship
commitment or breakdown, or the birth of children that
shake up your once settled life and demand that you create a new one. Because opportunities aren't equal or fair
for all, or because systems you might have hoped would

support or reward you fail to, and you have to find other ways forward. Or you reach that point in life when you find yourself face-to-face with the brevity and preciousness of your existence, and wonder how you might make the best of your time, or give something back. Whatever brought you here has seeded that most vital of questions: 'How do I want to live my life now?' Where you once knew the path, you now feel lost.

Pause here. Read that first sentence again. I want you to see feeling lost – uncomfortable as it might be – not as a personal deficiency deserving judgement or a fix but as an indication you are living your life *right*. I am sorry that you feel lost. I have been there myself and know that the experience can feel difficult and the question of what to do with your life can seem overwhelming. I have worked for years with people in the same situation as you. Not everyone can have personal sessions with a coach, so I have written this book because I hope to share with you what will help move you past where you are now to what might be possible next. You might not be able to see it yet but it is there, waiting for you. Right now, you only have my word for it. I ask you to trust me when I say that although you might *feel* something is wrong with you, nothing *is* wrong.

You are standing at a threshold – a place between the path you have been following and the choice to find another. You sense there is something more: more potential, more to discover, more to give to your life, your relationships, your work and to the world, more of *you*, but the way forward isn't clear. You're ready to find your own path.

You're not alone. As well as being a guide to help you find it, this book includes stories of people who have crossed this threshold and found their own meaningful path by changing their lives to fulfil more of their potential, to be more authentic – their lives aligned with who they are on the inside, making a positive impact in the time they have.

Eva is typical. In her mid-thirties at the time, she came to me because she felt stuck in her current life. She had overcome a great deal to get to where she was – redundancy, bad relationships, miscarriages and poor health – and she now had a job, a loving partner and a child. Yet she sensed that she had more to give, more potential to discover and bring into her life, and a greater contribution to make, but she wasn't sure what it was or how she would go about finding out and putting it into action.

'Is this it?' she wondered. 'Do I just keep my head down, swallow how I feel, and be grateful?'

After a few sessions working together, a shift happened. Using the processes and practices in this book, she realized what was important and meaningful to her and what got in the way of putting it into action; she tackled those obstacles and took steps to change her life. It wasn't the journey she was expecting. She realized what all my clients realize: what she was looking for wasn't a new job title or more pay but a more meaningful life – one in which she was creating her path, rather than accepting what was offered to her. You're going to discover her story later.

Feeling grateful for the life we have doesn't mean that

we can't make changes. While gratitude is important for our well-being, if we use it to smother or avoid the need or desire to make changes in our lives that would make them more meaningful, then we never allow a part of ourselves to speak. In this book, we're going to do just that.

Eva's realization was gradual, and came as a result of naturally growing and maturing. Once she had learned how to be an 'adult' in the world – socially successful, paying bills, having a committed relationship and becoming a parent – she found that the work that had made her happy when she was in her twenties no longer fulfilled her, and that there was more potential she now wanted to explore. Psychologists see our lives as having stages. In First Adulthood, we learn how to be successful in the world; in Second Adulthood, we yearn for greater authenticity and meaning in our lives. (For more on life stages, see Appendix 1.) This is why if you are feeling stuck, it doesn't mean there is anything wrong with you but that you are naturally maturing.

But sometimes we get thrown from the path we were following, and have to create a new one. Although we might wish it were otherwise, life doesn't run in a straight line but includes change and adversities, which demand we take a different direction. I invited several other people, as well as clients, to tell me how they found their own path, and they told stories of just such choices. Mia is one of them. An elegant, thoughtful teacher and dancer in her forties, she had to forge a different life for herself when she unexpectedly lost her work and home during the Covid-19 pandemic. Another, Charley, a bright and soulful woman, now in her thirties, is a former military officer. She left the forces by choice, but she witnessed many ex-colleagues who, on being routinely discharged after years of service, felt they had been cast out of the only institution in which their lives had had meaning. As she described it, even though they knew the end of their military service was coming, some remained anchored in the past, looking back with a sense of loss rather than forward with one of potential. Those who broke out of this found new ways forward that brought them new sources of meaning.

We are living within systems that are often unfair and don't offer opportunities equally. I want to introduce you to Devon, a warm and spiritually grounded man in his sixties, full of life, with a sense of wonder and exploration, who also offered his story. He was one of a trailblazing generation of black actors in the 1970s and '80s. But he had to struggle with not being asked to read for parts. Because of systemic prejudice, he and others have been overlooked for opportunities, promotions or roles. Faced with exhaustion, frustration, hardship or lack of fulfilment, they found other routes to meaning in their lives.

You're going to hear more about the stories of Eva, Mia, Charley, Devon and others, and how they found their own paths. See them as people who have gone before you, and are championing you, who believe that you can fulfil more of your potential, no matter where you are now. They have their hands on your back to support you.

Ageing can also bring you to the threshold of making a choice about how you want to live your life. If you are living your life right, then, sooner or later, you'll become aware that your lifespan is finite, and you may ask yourself what you want to do with the time you have left. As I write, I am experiencing shock at how I have suddenly become a middle-aged woman with fewer years ahead than behind me. Growing old is a privilege my birth mother didn't have but, if you're not there yet, I can only say it's not for cissies, though to me it is in many ways wonderful, not least because now I focus more on what's important and have perspective on how I want to live the remainder of my life. Middle age definitely brings you to the threshold, with a few creaking joints the least of your challenges. If this is you, then I am here with you, as are others in this book. My hand is on your back, even if it has more wrinkles than a few years ago.

However you come to find yourself at the threshold, remember you are not alone. I have been there. Many before you have found themselves at the same place, multitudes are here with you now, and countless more will reach it at some point in the future.* What matters now is what you do about it.

At this threshold, when faced with a choice to find your own path, I ask you to consider questions different

* Post-Covid, for instance, polls revealed that huge numbers of people reconsidered the major sources of meaning in their lives, such as what they do, where they live and whom they love. Over three-quarters of people in the UK re-evaluated their lives (YouGov); worldwide, forty per cent of workers planned to leave their employer (Microsoft Work Trend Index); and divorce lawyers saw triple-digit growth in enquiries (Stewarts).

from 'How can I be successful?' – based on how much money you make, what you own, your job title, your social media followers, where you live or what your social or romantic life looks like. Here, ask, 'Who am I really? How can I live an authentic life – one true to me, rather than the one I am expected to live?' Your touchstone is that to explore this you become more yourself.

The Threshold

I would be lying if I told you this is going to be easy. The root of the word 'threshold' comes from *thresh* or *thrash*, and it describes the place where grain would be separated from the chaff. This doesn't happen without a good shake. When you cross the threshold, you separate from social and cultural scripts about what you *should* be and do. You start a conversation with your deeper self – to find out who you really are on the inside. That's a brave thing to do, because the scripts are in many ways reassuring and rewarding, and there's no guarantee that what comes next can offer you the same external validation. Tuning in to the inner voice of your deeper self can also be tough because often it appears as physical, emotional or spiritual distress, and who wants to listen to that when you can avoid or anaesthetize it? Distress lets you know there's action required but doesn't offer a constructive way forward.

Here's how it spoke to Eric, now aged fifty, who as a younger man had a successful career as a top salesperson, with a marriage, children, and a big house with a four-wheel drive parked in front of it.

'I just can't keep doing this.'

A self-made man, he had been the poster boy for success. But he had become overweight, he felt his sexuality was repressed by family and church, and his marriage was falling apart. Once he decided to cross the threshold and change his life by being healthier, developing his spirituality and accepting his sexual nature, he discovered that as he became more the person he had the potential to be, his wife felt resentful. He could have chosen to return to being the version of himself that was acceptable to others, but as he said, 'In order to please an external rather than my own internal authority, I would have to lie. And the juice wasn't worth the squeeze.'

Crossing that threshold had huge consequences for him and others for whom he cared greatly, but he had faith it would be best for all of them. He left his church, his marriage and, eventually, his full-time sales career. Without knowing what his future would look like, he had to – as he puts it – 'jump into the chasm' and find his path. You'll also hear more about that later.

Your own life changes may not need to be as dramatic as Eric's. But however you found yourself here, you'll know you are at this threshold when you have a choice:

- to continue to live or try to go back to the life you know, numbing or ignoring the pain and frustration of inauthenticity;
- to hunt for something outside yourself – another job, relationship, location, friendship group or fitness regime – in the hope that it holds the promise of a more meaningful life, rather than

going inwards to discover what might be
meaningful to you first; or

- to explore who you are now and what you care
about, let go of some ways of being that feel
fixed, known and safe, but that no longer serve
you, and embark on the journey of a more
meaningful, authentic path.

Many people choose the first two options, for lots of
reasons. But here you are with this book in your hand.
What you might be sensing, but don't yet know, is what
I aim to help you discover in the course of this book.
You are bigger on the inside. Within you is potential
waiting for you to let it speak. This is the call you are
hearing. The upcoming act of your life is what you do
and become next. But to find it, you'll have to tackle
what gets in the way.

What Gets in the Way

Small wonder that we need some support to get across
the threshold and find our own path. As clients, inter-
viewees for this book and I have discovered, powerful
internal and external forces are very invested in our
remaining where we are.

We naturally need physical and material security and
safety. For a lot of us, day-to-day life is about surviving.
When you urgently need a place to live, to pay your bills
or to recover from a health crisis, finding your own path
can seem like a luxury, and that's understandable. When I

had no money and was homeless, getting those basic needs covered was my priority, and it will be the same for anyone. Also, uncertainty is psychologically challenging to manage and we sometimes understandably prefer choices that lower our anxiety by offering security, even if that means sacrificing an option that might be more fulfilling.

We built our old lives partly for psychological and social safety, and trying to create change will provoke intentionally protective, but sabotaging, internal mechanisms. What we know forms our comfort zone, and inner critics and saboteurs will defend this territory against the unknown, and make it sound like a sensible place to stay.

At the same time, our cultures, communities, families and even loved ones transmit powerful messages about the 'right' way to live, and it's frightening to think that we face their rejection and condemnation if we don't live our lives the way they think we should. Every day we receive images of what our lives ought to look like from advertising, media and social media, which induce discontent and longings for escape or a quick-click fix. Our economic model is reliant upon our consumption of products and services that promise to relieve the anxiety and dissatisfaction these images generate. At the same time, our 24/7 engagement in manufactured outrage spikes counterfeit aliveness. We are constantly distracted. When we are streaming boxsets, scrolling social media, bombarded with a 24-hour news cycle, trying to get everything done and plan the next weekend, we might be chasing fleeting experiences of happiness, relief or accomplishment, but do we pause enough to ask, 'Am I

living the life I truly want to live? Do I feel it's meaningful?' And do we do anything about it if we're not sure?
Why would that matter anyway?

Why Finding Your Own Path Matters

Answering the call to find a meaningful, authentic path in
life has a number of powerful benefits that aren't dependent on material or external measures of success.

1. Your sense of happiness and achievement
   emerges from a deeper sense of fulfilment
   within, rather than depending on external
   stimulation or validation. Living others' scripts,
   chasing fleeting happiness or momentary
   achievement can still leave you dissatisfied and
   restless in the long term.
2. Although you can't always choose what life
   throws at you, you have a sense of agency over
   how you respond, rather than being the passive
   recipient of a series of events. Don't you want
   to have a say in how your story unfolds?
3. You are better able to tolerate difficult feelings
   and challenges, which helps you deal with life's
   struggles and adversities.
4. Because of this, you can look back at your life
   and struggles, see how they made you the
   person you are now and feel a sense of
   acceptance and compassion for yourself and
   shared humanity with others.

5. It reduces the number and intensity of your regrets. The number-one regret people have at the end of their lives is that they did what others expected them to do, rather than living authentically.*

I hope that by the end of this book you'll be able to feel at least some of these benefits, and even add a few more. I invite you to heed the call to find your path and live a more meaningful life. It is calling you with good reason.

How This Book Can Help

This is a guide to the conversation we need to start with ourselves to create a more meaningful life, and to the ways we can start to put it into action. Here are my guiding principles, which will help you know what to expect.

This is a book for humans. We are not perfect; neither is anyone else. We feel vulnerable and frightened at times, and that's part of being human. We deserve compassion, not judgement. I also don't see us as machines that need fine-tuning to maximum optimization. Life isn't an endless conveyor belt of tasks we need to get on top of by being more productive and efficient. Trust me, on your last day on Earth, you won't be glad you emptied your email inbox weekly. What matters is not how much we do but doing the important things that bring meaning to our lives.

* Bronnie Ware, *The Top Five Regrets of the Dying* (2019).

This is a book that is relevant for all parts of your life. You can use it to focus on career, relationships or anything else. Your life is bigger than just one part of it.

Your hands are on the wheel. If this sounds scary, take heart. You have more power than you might realize. Right now, you need some help, and that's nothing to be ashamed of or worried about, it's normal. See this book as your guide, offering insights, tools, exercises and practices that will help you tackle fears and resistance, discover your path and take steps to steer along it.

We are all doing our best. I am not going to promise that creating a meaningful life requires only that you use the right formula, come up with a plan and execute it, as if being human doesn't come with fears, resistances and tendencies towards repeating patterns, and as if we live in a world in which opportunities are equal for all. I don't have a magic pill. The concept that we can simply dream it and then be it is laden with privilege. That's also why, in a later chapter, I focus on how we can raise our resilience when things don't go our way.

Having a more meaningful life is possible for all of us. We can get caught in the trap of having big, lofty notions of what a meaningful life is supposed to look like. What if we are not the ones to single-handedly save the rainforests, find a cure for cancer, write a great novel or develop an app that changes the world? What then? Does that mean our lives lack meaning? Absolutely not. Meaning is imbued by you in whatever you are being or doing. I just stepped outside to empty my bins and paused to hear a bird sing. I felt aware of how big and extraordinary the natural world is, and that was a meaningful moment for me. It's a choice I make in how to live my life, even in each ordinary moment.

We have an impact on others. No matter what we choose to be and do, or how we decide to show up and act, our choices impact not only our own lives but those of others too. In finding your own path, you inspire and support them to find their own.

You are not alone. It helps to know that there are others like you who found a way to live a more meaningful life. I have included my own story and those of clients and others, who have kindly given their permission. Most of the names have been changed, and some are composites of several people, but the issues are typical. Although the circumstances and stories may be different from yours, like you, we all found ourselves at a point where we needed to figure out how to change our lives. It took reflection, awareness, acceptance, permission, resilience and action, and that's what this book is going to help you with.

As a coach, I work with people to help them develop and follow through on plans for a more fulfilled life, and support them to identify and manage internal and external obstacles that arise. I am not a therapist or a healthcare professional; if you feel you need help from one of those, then please do this as soon as you can. I know how much therapy helped me. I'll include some information in the resource section at the end. In this book, I am interested in offering some guidance along the journey of this messy, precious, real human life to help you find your own path so that, at the end of your days, you can say, 'I lived the life I was meant to live. I brought the gifts of my whole self into my life, and I did my best.' If you are curious about embarking on this journey, then I hope this book will be of use. Don't just use it once, return to it whenever you need to. Given the demands and importance of the task, we all need some help.

Why I Wrote This Book

My own call to action came from two parallel journeys – professional and personal. Professionally, I have come to an insight. Although people often come to coaching or a course I facilitate with a presenting issue, such as a tricky boss, lack of work–life balance, a leadership challenge, the need to start again after illness or redundancy, or a desired solution in the form of a new job or a move to the country, what they really seek is *meaning*, which we can find when we create a path that aligns with

- *values* that we choose to live by – those inner integral beliefs and codes that guide us from within;
- and *purpose* that we devote our energy towards – the bigger picture that gives the preciousness of our lives meaning.

This insight, as well as many of the ideas, exercises and practices in this book, builds upon the work of others. I have received superb training from the founders and teachers of the Co-Active Training Institute, the Embodied Facilitator Course, the Earth Wisdom Teachings

Sacred Leadership Programme, the Embercombe Journey and others, who have influenced the exercises and approaches in this book, as have my own coaches, therapists, spiritual teachers and other guides to my emotional self-development. Behind this stand psychologists, neuroscientists, psychotherapists and generations of teachers, shamans and spiritual leaders who have handed down to us practices and ways of thinking and being that are truly useful, such as self-reflection, mindfulness, acceptance, nature connection and the integration of body and mind. It feels good to know that we're on solid ground when we are ready to stand up and start walking out of the woods. Tapping into the wisdom of those who have come before, my clients and I, along with many others, find practices and insights that work – not just for a quick fix that fades but for deep transformation that lasts.

Which brings me to my personal call-to-action. I have walked this path myself. I am still walking it. I sense I always will. Feeling lost at times is part of that path, not a separate sinkhole. I came to find myself in a dark wood in my early forties, lost not only in what I was doing in the world but also from myself. These are inextricably linked: if you don't know yourself better, you don't know what would give your life meaning. Because I am living my life right – growing, facing challenges and setbacks, aware that I am human and mortal – I still struggle at times, and need to make space to check in with myself and find and reconnect with my path. And when things don't go to plan, I still need to recover, learn and figure out what to do next. I don't need fixing, because I am not

broken – and neither are you, although it might feel like
that sometimes. I have written the guide I wish I had had,
and which I still need.

The Journey of the Book

Here's where we are going. Integrating what I have learned
and practised with myself and clients, I have structured
this book as a series of steps, although you may find that
you want to go to some chapters before others, depending
on what you need. For instance, if inner critics are making
it hard for you from the outset, read that chapter first, or
if your energy levels are too low to start, check out Chapter Six. I start with the inner work to help you get to know
yourself and put yourself in the driver's seat of your life,
and then we hit the road.

> *Step One: Separate from Old Scripts.* Spot and reduce
> the power of those internalized scripts and
> beliefs that hold you where you are.
> *Step Two: Make Space for Your Bigger Self.* Switch off
> autopilot, find space and time to connect with
> yourself at a deeper level and make more useful,
> conscious choices.
> *Step Three: Start the Conversation.* Connect to what
> really matters to you with some powerful self-
> reflection exercises.
> *Step Four: Build Your Compass.* Align your path with
> your integral, authentic beliefs or principles to
> feel more energized and motivated and to seek

out and attract more opportunities and people that share them.

Step Five: Shift Perspective and Let Go. One day will be your last, so — rather than collapse into nihilism or cling to the scripts of your youth — embrace the need to live your precious life with purpose, grace and integrity, focusing on what ultimately matters and letting go of what doesn't.

Step Six: Replenish Your Wells. Discover more about what drains or energizes your different wells of energy so you have the resources you need.

Step Seven: Make Peace with Inner Critics and Saboteurs. As you find your own path, build a healthy relationship with the parts of you that are going to get in your way, and get them out of the driving seat of your life.

Step Eight: Find Allies. Gather the inner and outer support you need.

Step Nine: Give Yourself Permission to Make Choices. Break through analysis-paralysis and perfectionism, using your heart and gut as well as your head.

Step Ten: Nurture Your Ideas and Put Them into Action. Purpose, nourish and strengthen your ideas and get moving with small experiments.

Step Eleven: Raise Your Resilience. Recover and grow from difficulties and setbacks.

Step Twelve: Tell Your Story. Tell your new story for yourself and for others, so that you can acknowledge how far you've come and be a guide for those who are ready to find their own path.

Get Ready to Start

You'll need a journal – somewhere you write down and review what you are discovering. Journalling here is not quite the same as keeping a diary in which you download and free-write whatever is going on in your life. It's a bit more structured than that. Within this book I have included:

Exercises for you to try, which will help you discover more about yourself, and which you can do more than once if needed. Use your journal to record what you learn so you can lock it in and remind yourself.

Practices to embed into your life regularly. Change happens through small choices that you make every day rather than one giant leap. Writing down their effects will help motivate you to continue.

Journal Questions to help you reflect. You can revisit these whenever you need to.

Research shows that, as well as increasing self-awareness, journalling can help improve our sense of self-efficacy or our belief that we can act in ways that will help us reach goals. Regular journalling can boost well-being and resilience and reduce anxiety. Even fifteen minutes a day has an effect. Writing helps us think better: when we write, we slow down and tease out those fast, tangled thoughts into something more manageable. Our thoughts often arrive like *millefeuille* – that flaky pastry slice which holds a thousand messy layers in one over-whelming mouthful. But when we write, it's as if we roll out the pastry of our thoughts and can reflect upon them with more distance. You can revisit the discoveries you record in your journal whenever you get stuck or lost. When you do, there's nothing wrong; it's part of the process. Gather yourself and reset. Turn your journal to a new page. Each day is a fresh opportunity.

As you prepare to embark on this journey, I invite you to pause and notice how you feel right now. I often ask new clients to notice their patterns or habits of thinking, feeling and doing, using a simple intuitive model of the seasons, inspired by embodiment teacher Mark Walsh. We're always noticing, not judging or shaming – which is important to remember throughout this book. Becoming more aware is great, because then you can make conscious choices.

Journal Questions

Open your journal and write a few notes about which of these seasons you can relate to (you can adjust this if you are in the southern hemisphere). Perhaps it's something completely different – if so, nice noticing!

> *Spring.* Perhaps you feel excited, ready to dive in at the beginning. Maybe you have a tendency to drop off later.
>
> *Summer.* You might feel more tentative at the beginning, but once you warm up, you love full

flow. Maybe you want every day to be great, but get disheartened when it's not always like that.

Autumn. Perhaps this is your pattern: as long as you have a book or a course, you feel great, but once you finish it, you drop off. Or maybe you rush to get to the end of each chapter so you can get to the harvest of results more quickly.

Winter. Perhaps you dread the times when nothing seems to be happening and you feel impatient for spring. Or maybe you enjoy the quiet isolation of self-reflection.

As I am going to remind you as you go along, there is no right or wrong, no way you *should* be. What is important is that you increase your awareness and accept yourself with compassion – after all, we are humans doing our best. Then, knowing what you do about yourself, choose what you want to be and do – this is how you find your own path.

Further Journal Questions

Take a moment now to explore these questions in your journal:

- What do you want from this book?
- What patterns or habits of thinking, feeling and doing might get in the way?
- What might help and what would you like to try?
- How will you remind yourself of this?

We don't credit ourselves enough with the courage it takes to find our own path. I stand here at the threshold, between the life you have been living and the life that's possible, and welcome you with open arms and a whole heart. Thank you for trusting in me, and in yourself. You are just at the beginning of the next great adventure. It's called the rest of your life.

1. Separate from Old Scripts

Imagine you are standing lost in a wood. It's dark and there isn't a path you can see. You want to get out of here and be on a path you find fulfilling, but how will you get there, and where would that be? You don't yet have a direction or a map. You feel stuck. In this book, I aim to help you find yourself again, and to create a new path in life in which how you show up in the world is in alignment with who you are now, and more meaningful because of that. From where you are now to where you want to be there are three stages. The first is getting unstuck by *separating* from where you are currently, so you can get moving. The second is the *transition* through the wood, where you get your bearings and try to find or create a way for yourself. Most of this book is going to give you tools, insights, practices and exercises that will help you through this stage. Finally, you *incorporate* all you have learned and put it into action in your life so that you can walk your path. Reading this book alone isn't enough – so be prepared to do the work. This first chapter and the next are about separating from what holds you where you are now, so you can start your journey. Right now, at the beginning, I am going to stand alongside you in the wood, and together we're going to take a look at the old inner scripts and stories by which you are currently living your life – which may be stopping you from finding your own more authentic path – lessening their power over you just enough that you can start to move.

How to Know You Are Ready to Find Your Own Path

When we follow the scripts of who we are supposed to be and what we are supposed to do with our lives, somewhere along the way we can lose ourselves. But, far from being a sign of failure, knowing you are lost is the vital first line of the story you are going to start writing yourself. When you separate yourself from your old life and start to consider what would feel more meaningful, you can see the ways in which you confuse what you have or don't have – your achievements, wealth, possessions, roles and statuses – with who you actually are. Remember the story of Eric? He reached a point when he realized who he was didn't fit the life he had created for himself. Although his life was successful in the ways listed above, unfulfilled potential and the longing to live his truth started knocking on his door from within, asking for permission to speak. That moment of realizing he couldn't go on – as he vividly put it, that the juice wasn't worth the squeeze – was an *initiation*. This is that moment when you find yourself at a threshold, facing the choice to find a way out of the life you have been living and your attachment to it, and create your own path.

There are other ways we find ourselves at that threshold. Your initiation may be the realization that you want to give something back, as interviewee Bruce, now in his early forties, told me. He had built a stable career as an accountant. But around his fortieth birthday, his perspective shifted. 'I realized that I was lining my employers' pockets and paying my bills, but it wasn't really doing anything better for society. I wanted to do something that had an impact outside of my sphere.'

For some, life events carry them to the threshold. Here are the initiation moments of a few of the people whose stories you'll hear more of in this book. You have already met Devon, the actor, who ran into financial troubles he had to stop avoiding and begin to face. Dancer and teacher Mia had a different initiation – a series, in fact, which can be common. Her son left for university, and then, during the Covid-19 pandemic, she lost her home and the work that was so tied to her previous identity. If this wasn't enough, she then contracted a serious foot infection, which meant it was unlikely she could return to dance in the way she had before. Lying in bed after surgery, she made some big decisions. Meet Alana, whose life changed when she received a cancer diagnosis. In Chapter Five, you'll discover more about the journey her initiation started, and how she lives her life now.

Others found themselves let down by a system they thought would give them rewards if they worked hard enough. I am thinking of Charley, the former military officer you have already met. She had already sensed a small internal voice saying there might be something else out there to explore.

'I said to myself, "Let's see if I get promoted before I decide what to do." But I didn't, even though I had lots of recommendations. I was like, "Quite frankly, I am not investing another decade of my life playing the game."'

This was her initiation moment. It came for me as a panic attack. It might come for you in the form of aching dissatisfaction or symptoms such as pain, illness or anxiety and depression, or excitement at a new possibility of which you catch a glimpse. It can even arrive in the form of a dream, another way – like illness or anxiety – that what is buried within us can make its presence felt.

Say hello to Adam, a hearty and generous games developer. He founded a business that ran into trouble and he was made redundant after it was bought out. Not a great experience, but one that set him on a different path. The night he was fired, Adam awoke at 3 a.m. after such a dream, which woke him in more ways than one. He realized he was longing for something he had not yet discovered.

'In my dream, I was in this apartment block, trying to find a party. I could hear it as I was walking up the stairwells. It's dark, and eventually I find this open door. There's a lady with a green face sat at a school desk, and I'm like, "Is this where the party is? I really want to go to the party." And then I woke up.'

The next day, he intuitively knew he had to ask for help from some local people who held nature-based ceremonies. They agreed to take him to the woods nearby and make some offerings to the spirit of nature, which they told him was sometimes represented as a green lady. He did a double-take, and took it as a sign he was on the right path.

Maybe you have received other signs that it's time for you to find your own path. You might even experience a 'cosmic flirt' as your own initiation, when something seems to leap out from the background noise and send you a message you need to hear right now.

Let me introduce you to writer Yasmin Khan, who agreed that I could use her real name. She felt a great sense of purpose in her old job, but when she burned out, she had to face the prospect of leaving it. Her own initiation came when, one day, she saw something on a poster that helped her realize that her current struggles were part of a bigger process of change, rather than a sign of failure.

'This is a true story of synchronicity. I was having coffee and feeling a real crisis because I was so tied into this identity of this job that I loved. I looked up, and there was this poster on the wall with a quote that said, sometimes on the way to the dream, you get lost and find a better one. And I was just like, yes!'

She still keeps a photo of that poster to remind and nourish her.

What's your initiation? What led you to pick up this book? It's an important part of your story, and one to remind yourself of, especially in those moments when you feel the temptation to turn back.

Journal Questions

Take a moment to journal:

- How do I know I am ready to find my own path?
- What has led me to this moment?
- How do I feel?

- What's important to me about how I feel right now?

Whatever brought you to this point, you're ready to answer the call to change your life.

But where do you start? If it was easy to hear the initiation call to change your life and immediately answer, then nobody would need life coaches. Changing your life is hard because it is underpinned by external social or out-of-date scripts that we cling to as core beliefs or inner stories about how the world is and how we are. You can change aspects of your life – your job, your partner, your fitness regime, your location, for instance – and still follow those scripts.

Let me take the back off the television set of my own life. At thirty, I changed my career path from being an academic to working in the corporate world, and moved from New York, where I had been studying for five years, to London, a city where I had never lived before. Huge change on the outside. But on the inside, I was still following the path that was unfolding in front of me, dictated to me by the end of my PhD and my US visa, the job offers I received – or didn't, and my belief that whether it was the academic or corporate ladder, it was probably better to be on a ladder than not.

I want to emphasize that there's nothing wrong with any of this. I learned a great deal that serves me very well now, met wonderful people and had some terrific experiences and achievements of which I am genuinely proud. I don't trash my past or judge myself for it, and, if you can relate, I invite you to take your hand off the self-criticism button. I didn't know then what I know now. In this book, I am meeting you in the woods, at the place where you feel lost, and I am inviting you to change your life at a deeper level – to look at the buried scripts that govern your life and decide whether they are true for you or serve you any more. If you want your life to be more meaningful, you need to be true to yourself, rather than seeking the acceptance and approval of others, and performing and hiding behind masks – as I can now see I was. This can feel hard, and the temptation to turn back can be great. Following these scripts may have helped us to be successful so far. Fear of loss exerts a massive and opposite pull on us as we try to move forward. Studies show that it can even motivate us more than hope of gain. But unless you can free yourself from these scripts – even a little – it's hard to see what you might do next. Your first step is to start to notice the scripts from which you need to separate.

Start to Notice the Scripts Running Your Life

Like the proverbial fish that doesn't know it's swimming in water, your life so far has been shaped by scripts so internalized, integrated and normalized into core beliefs or stories that you might not even be able to see them. Here's an exercise to help you spot them. We're going to go hunting for the 'shoulds' in your life. When I coach, I hold a figurative butterfly net, ready to catch the little critters, which pop up all over my conversations with clients.

Exercise: Revealing the Scripts

Try finishing some of these sentences with the first thing that comes to mind:

- At my age, I should . . .
- My partner/family thinks I should . . .
- I should do . . . at weekends.
- Now I am a . . . I should . . .
- I should spend my time . . .
- I should wear . . .
- I should earn . . .
- I should feel . . .
- I should do . . . with my income.
- I should . . . with my children.
- My life should . . .

Please feel free to add your own 'shoulds'; catch them throughout your day and skewer them on a pin by writing them down in your journal. Approach them with a vibrant curiosity, rather than judgement. Later I'll give you some questions to help explore them.

Our 'shoulds' are not all necessarily bad or wrong – for instance, I *should* pay taxes, call my dad on his birthday and resist that second helping of dessert – but some may not align with who you are or serve your life any more. Catching and separating yourself from them is important because the implicit or explicit stories you tell yourself have a great impact on your life. Some of them run your life in ways that block you from seeing what else might be possible and finding your own path.

It helps to see 'shoulds' as stories or scripts, like an underlying operating system programmed into your computer, managing your life in the background. These stories might not be 100 per cent true all the time, some may be beliefs rather than facts, but in some ways they may have helped you to operate successfully in the world, to be approved of and liked, and to belong. This is why we hold on to them fiercely and what makes them so sticky. Often unconsciously, we *choose* to live by them, because, in some way, there's what therapists call a *pay-off* or reward,* and it's important to understand what these are, so we can question their truth or value to us, to see if the juice really is worth the squeeze.

Here's an example of exposing such a script or story and its pay-off. I met my client Graham in the lobby of a smart hotel – the type where a pianist murders a selection of easy listening classics. He is a charming middle-aged man looking to step away from the day-to-day responsibilities of running his own business to focus on what comes next. Avuncular, warm and thoughtful, he always asks me if I have eaten, and, if not, would I like lunch or afternoon tea? This, as we shall see, is part of the issue. I ask him to tell me about what he needs today from coaching, and he starts with 'we', meaning his business and all the people in it. I ask him to begin again, this time starting with what *he* needs.

* If you'd like to understand more about pay-offs, then I recommend reading existential psychotherapist Irvin Yalom's wonderful books *The Gift of Therapy* (2001) and *Love's Executioner* (1989).

'Of course,' he replies, before saying, 'What we need –'

I interrupt. 'Could you start the next sentence with "*I* need", rather than "we"?'

He pauses and rolls his eyes up towards the roof, struggling to rearrange the underpinning of not just *what* he thinks but *how* he thinks.

'Okay,' he slowly pronounces with effort, '*I . . . need . . . more . . . space.*'

I encourage him to take the stabilizers off.

'I need time for myself. I need something for me.'

He recoils to a stop.

'This feels wrong . . . and . . .' I give him a few seconds. 'Good, great, actually. But also wrong.'

An old unconscious internalized script is rubbing up against a new possibility, and now is the perfect moment to expose it.

'What's coming up that says it's wrong?' I ask.

'It feels selfish. I should think of other people, not myself.'

There it is – a powerful script about being 'good': you need to think of others and always put their needs before your own, otherwise you are selfish and not a good person. Graham has been living inside this script for so long that he struggles even to think of or express his own needs. He is sacrificing them on the altar of seeing himself as a good person (his pay-off), as if there is a zero-sum game at play here – you can't be a good person *and* think of your own needs – because that's what this script says. Using the simple statement 'I need' is a revelation to Graham, as it might be for you.

We create pay-offs unconsciously. When we resist change, we collect the pay-off of avoiding uncertainty, judgement, failure, the consequences of success, such as increased responsibility or scrutiny, for instance, and uncomfortable feelings like guilt for being 'selfish', which become scapegoats for not taking action. My role is to help Graham – and you – notice the old scripts and pay-offs which keep us stuck.

As a rule for this journey, when you feel stuck, I invite you to become curious, rather than judgemental. It could be a signal that an underlying script has been activated, and here's a great opportunity to notice it. By becoming curious and compassionate about our scripts, rather than accepting them as inviolable, we open them out enough to allow air and light into what seems like a dark, closed room, and see other possibilities. When we don't, we stay in ruts which shape what we understand is happening in any given moment and thus our range of responses. If you believe that thinking about yourself is selfish, then you'll find it hard. New stories, paths, pay-offs and ways to live our lives that better serve us can emerge when we stop our investment in old ones.

Not all of our beliefs are internalized scripts handed to us wholesale by our culture. When faced with situations in which we can't or don't understand why things happen, we often make up a story to make sense of it all. It's as if our confusion rises up and a script dives down to hook it and reel it in. Let's notice some of these stories, reveal them as possible fictions, start to unhook ourselves and then rewrite them.

Exercise: Identifying and Challenging Core Beliefs

As you read this list of beliefs, notice any strong reactions in your body, such as a sinking feeling, faster-beating heart or desire to do something else. That could be the hook in you, so go gently. Rather than getting lost or stuck in your feelings, see your reactions as helpful signals that this story is indeed one of your own. Please write any that are your own in your journal.

- I need to be perfect to be valued.
- Nobody wants to date/hire people over forty.
- I am unlovable.
- If I love someone, they will hurt me.
- If I get something wrong, my children will be damaged forever.
- Good guys come last.
- You can't trust people.

This is a list of examples, and you may have other core beliefs. If so please add them along with any of the above to a list in your journal. Keep some space free for any more that you notice in future.

Once you have unearthed them, take them along with the 'shoulds' you uncovered earlier and unpack them with a few powerful questions.

- How do I benefit by seeing things this way?
- What is the cost?
- Is it totally true in every case?

- What might be another way of seeing this?
- What might I gain through seeing this another way?

Tempting though it might be to beat yourself up for your internalized scripts and beliefs, don't be hard on yourself. Some may have been forged aeons ago with good reason – inherited social rules to help us to co-operate together in communities rather than fighting each other (for instance, I need to think of other people). Others when you were looking for social approval and its benefits (if I work late, I will be valued). Have a little non-judgemental understanding of their original purpose, but be ready to uproot them to build new, more useful foundations for your life.

From time to time, a client will look at me in astonishment when I tell them that I need to do the same work I invite them to do, such as the questions above. I suspect there's a script dangling around that life coaches have it all figured out and now exist in a state of enlightenment, immune to scripts and stories. Not in the least. When I wrote 'I am unlovable', something in my chest turned liquid. It was for years a core belief of mine, from which I still sometimes need to unhook. Every time a relationship failed, every time I didn't get a job I wanted or lost one, and even at times when I walked into a room, said hello and no one responded, I reread and reinscribed it deeper as a fundamental truth about myself. How else to explain the disappointments in my life?

My friends assured me they loved me. I did have other jobs and relationships. Yet this belief persisted. Why would I hold on to it? After all, it's painful. What could possibly be the pay-off? In an uncertain world, a core belief gives us an anchor or safe harbour. It offers us a lifebelt when the world seems chaotic and ambiguous, and avoids all the energy-consuming examination of the alternatives. This one was mine. It was one certain thing to which I could cling in the chaos of unimaginable loss at a very early age when my mother died. When you are very young, before you have developed a sense of yourself separate from others, it seems as if everything is about you. You believe that if bad things happen, they happen because of you. As a two-year old, unable to conceptualize death, I believed my mother had left me because I was unlovable, and in holding on to this and revisiting it with every disappointment, I could somehow retrieve her again, if not in person then through the belief I created when I lost her. It was no use saying this was silly. Would you call a two-year-old silly for being two? Yet this is what we do when we judge ourselves for those old stories and core beliefs, and it's why we need to sit next to them with curiosity and compassion, as we would a small child.

When we do so, we can start to loosen their grip and see how we might rewrite them in ways that can help us find another, more useful and truer foundation for our path. I'll use my own example to show how you can do this yourself through the questions above:

- How do I benefit by believing I am unlovable?
  - Because if I believe it, then I never have to expect or hope I will be loved. If I don't hope

to be loved, I won't risk being abandoned
again.

- What is the cost?
  - The opportunity to be loved for who I am, and to know I am.
- Is it totally true in every case?
  - No, my friends and family love me. They are not entirely crazy.
- How else might I see it?
  - My mother loved me very much, so much so that when she knew she was dying, she made sure I would be taken care of by a family who loved me.
- What might I gain through seeing my story like this?
  - If I believe I am lovable, I can appreciate not only her love for me but also let in the love of others. If I don't receive the love and acceptance I want, I can understand that it's not about me and so be more authentically vulnerable, courageous and resilient.

As I mentioned, this old core belief still flares up at times, as your own might, even after doing this exercise, so don't judge yourself if this happens to you too. As with many of the exercises and practices in the book, this isn't a once-and-done thing, like taking a magic pill. Scripts and stories are persistent, wired in, and you will need to catch them and revisit this exercise throughout your life. I know that when I do, I become able to write a new story that nourishes and supports me on my path. It's human to have these scripts and challenging them is work that's rarely finished. It's like weeding a garden, turning over the soil and creating new space and conditions for growth. We have to do it when needed. With practice, you'll find it gets easier.

Living Your Whole Life

You have been reading the script, now it's time to start to write your own. You have started to separate from the old scripts and beliefs that no longer serve you, the next chapter is going to help you create the space for a new, more authentic and meaningful story by switching off autopilot, and the rest of this book is going to help you out of the woods to write that story and find your own path. Right now, at the beginning of this journey, it's only natural it feels uncertain and challenging, as this new future is not yet solid enough to place a foot on, and it's another reason why your old stories and life will call you back to familiar ground with urgency. Your journey may well at times also include plateaus and dead ends.

If that sounds frightening, at this beginning, I ask you to bear the sometimes uncomfortable feelings which will arise in any transition, and to strengthen your 'negative capability', as the poet John Keats called the ability to be willing to accept uncertainty, doubt and the unknown. As my client Maria said, having left a long-term academic career and relationship, 'Know that you can live through the fear. It's not going to kill you.' These aren't just fine words, spoken in her rich New York accent; she knows what she's talking about, as her story later will demonstrate.

When our negative capability is low, we can all have a tendency to grasp for quick answers. Truth is, life isn't a problem that needs solving. You are finding a path, not aiming for a good grade in a test. Try not to grasp for quick solutions as a way of avoiding the discomfort of not knowing what your path might look like yet. Take your guidance from the Austrian-Hungarian poet Rainer Maria Rilke, who advised going inwards and living the questions.* As he said, you may then discover that one day you are living your answers. The question you are going to explore in this book is 'How can I find my own path and live a life that's meaningful to me?' It is an invitation into a rich journey of discovery and expansion – and you are giving it to yourself.

We naturally seek to grow and flourish, to live the breadth of our lives, rather than tread a narrow, pre-scribed route. I often take a walk in nature for inspiration, especially when I notice I am living too much in my head, seeking answers and solutions, overwhelmed by the demands and distractions of modern life. One of my favourite places to rest is under a great tree. I look up and see how the trunk branches out into a canopy and the stem of a leaf bursts into colourful fruiting vibrancy. We sometimes forget that we ourselves are a part of nature. Whatever your initiation was, whatever brought you to your threshold, there is a seed in you that yearns to grow. As we go forward in this book, you're going to nourish it.

* *Letters to a Young Poet* (1929).

2. Make Space for Your Bigger Self

I sit at my desk peering at the screen, where I can see my coaching client hundreds of miles away through the magic that is live internet video. Jan's head is lowered, as she awaits her punishment. At the end of our last session, she agreed to start decluttering her home as the first step towards building a new act in her life. She didn't, and now she is expecting me to turn into Fiona, Bringer of Judgement. That's not the business I'm in. I am, however, curious. What happened? She has an insight. For most of her day she does things for others, and has no time or space for herself. 'Congratulations!' I beam. Her face scrunches with confusion – this was not the response she expected. But this insight is a major landmark. Without noticing what's holding us back, and then unhooking ourselves from it – as we started to explore in the previous chapter – we can't move forward.

Her issue is common. Each day thousands of automatic choices hold us tight in our current lives.* In the previous chapter, you started to explore the scripts and stories that are holding you back; this chapter will help you open up enough space to write a story of your own. It's time to switch off autopilot through mindful awareness and stress regulation, so you can do the reflection

---

* We make 35,000 decisions a day, according to some sources.

and practices that will help you find your own path, and to make sure that it is based on your own active choices, rather than automatic reactions. When you do, you'll discover there was always more of you than there is on automatic, living on the surface of your life, and it's waiting to be called upon. This chapter covers powerful practices to help you reach in and find it.

I always start with new clients by asking them when they are going to make time to reflect and practise what they are learning, as 99 per cent of self-development happens outside the coaching hour – and once you put down this book. The novelist Virginia Woolf famously said we need a room of one's own to write. I say you need an hour a day to yourself to change your life.

Remember Devon, the man now in his sixties, who started out as an actor? He has changed his life from one in which he relied on fleeting gain of money to feel happy to one in which his material worth is built on a solid foundation of self-worth. He and I agree about what it takes to start to change your life from lived experience.

'It takes discipline. It's about every single day having a place or a time you set aside to really reflect on your life, and to remind yourself of all the potential that there is within it until it becomes unequivocally yours.'

Yet today, this is a revolutionary requirement. We have simply lost the ability to have time to ourselves to reflect. If Woolf was around today, she might sit in that room scrolling the internet and answering emails. If I didn't switch notifications off (a simple practice I recommend), I would be constantly interrupted and pulled away from myself by pop-ups and pings. If I didn't hold boundaries and say no, my internalized scripts and 'shoulds' would cause me to sacrifice my time on the altar of their insidious imperatives. Unless we take action, we lose a quality of attention towards our deeper selves that we need.

We live a great deal on the surface of our lives, held there by our habits, shortcuts, busyness, the search for instant gratification, and 'shoulds'. The stress that results falls across our lives like a screen, blocking our view of ourselves and what we could be and do instead. As a consequence, we stay small – what I call the 'Little I' – spending our precious lives without fulfilling our potential to live more authentically and meaningfully. Our first step towards changing this is to open up space to have a conversation with our 'Big I' – the part that encompasses our deeper longings and potential.

Here's my analogy for our deeper Big I selves. I once sat still in a wood in the Scottish mizzle. On hearing a slight sound, I raised my eyes to see a young deer close by. As I held my breath at the glorious sight, my phone buzzed and the deer bounded away into the trees. My deeper self is like this wild and shy creature, which flees from the noise of everyday life. We need to cultivate a relationship with it to understand what our own path might be and put it into action.

The Battle for Your Attention

Your first step is to create some quality time and space for yourself. You can't do that unless you are aware of how you currently use your time.

Exercise: The Awareness Diary

Take your journal and fill a page with your diary for one day, with hours from midnight to midnight. Include any activities and tasks you have planned.

Record how you *actually* spend your time as you experience it – our memories are poor at recalling what we did later. Note anything you did automatically or habitually.

Here's what my diary looks like for the early part of today:

4 a.m.: Woke, toilet, went back to bed. Checked news and social media (automatic).

4.30 a.m.: Went back to sleep.

6.45 a.m.: Woke. Switched on radio and dozed in bed half-listening (habit).

7.15 a.m.: Made a cup of tea (good habit), brought it back to bed (not great). Checked news and social media (habit).

7.45 a.m.: Ruminated on why my friend hasn't responded to my message. Felt worried (habit).

8 a.m.: Had shower, etc. (habit – a useful one).

There's nothing wrong here, unless you are attached to a notion that life coaches rise at 5 a.m. for an hour's meditation, followed by an ice bath. But when you write your diary, you may start to notice – as I did – plenty of habitual, not useful activities that *entrance* us, as if we fall under a spell of mindless doing, thinking and feeling that keeps us away from deeper reflection or thoughtful choice about better Big I things we could be doing. We can beat ourselves up for this, but we are human, and for much for our lives we are all on automatic, partly because of how our brains work.

Ironically for an organ we associate with thought, our brains are incredibly good at not thinking. Thinking takes precious energy, so having an automatic energy-saving system can be a great advantage, but is less so when you are trying to find a new path in life. It's not a personal failing, but it is something we can notice and change to clamber out of the automatic Little I rut of our lives. It helps to understand five ways being human makes this harder.

1. Habits

Your brain uploads useful and repeated activities into habits, some of which you need to override. All day you do things without much deep thinking or conscious processing. For instance, when you cross a road, you can do it quickly, as your brain took in all you learned about how to do it safely when you were a child and automated it to be efficient. But other automatic habits aren't so helpful. We spend more time than we know is good for us scrolling the web, for example. If you are like me, you'll also spend a lot of time worrying, which is sometimes useful, but other times not – a handy distinction I wish my brain made more often. The more we scroll or worry, the more the brain uploads it to automatic habit, and this leaves us with a problem. Our habits get in the way of us seeing things freshly and numb us to our own experience. We become less mindful, less aware of what's going on around us and within us, and so less able to make choices that aren't on autopilot. Ever started to cross a road, only to be nearly sideswiped by a bike? Ever had good intentions to do something for yourself, only to be pulled down another internet rabbit hole? As you went about your daily routine, did you ever fail to notice that you were becoming increasingly unhappy in a job or a relationship – or that someone else was? As I do with clients, I ask you to slow down and pause. Then you can ask yourself two important questions in order to switch autopilot off and turn on the more mindful and aware part of yourself.

- What would be useful right now?
- What do I *choose* to be and do in this moment?

Later in this chapter, I have a couple of great practices for mindful awareness and stress regulation to help you create that pause and open out just enough space to act from choice rather than habit. But first, let's take a look at what else creates the need to override automatic at times.

2. Shortcuts

Our brains like shortcuts. They take in as little information as they need to make an educated guess and then generalize. We do this in every area of our lives, and those shortcuts harden into the fixed, automatic way we see the world, affecting how we act in it. Shortcuts create our perception of reality and keep us on our old paths. Ever walked into a room and instantly assumed that your presentation or your date is going to go badly? There might be another story you could tell. Ever quickly said yes to something to avoid the negative consequences of saying no, when those consequences might not ever appear? When you spot what might be a shortcut assumption, ask yourself the following:

Journal Questions

- Am I making an assumption here?
- Is this the only possible way of seeing this?
- How else could I see this?

Here's an example from my casebook. In her early thirties, my client Rachel wanted to change her life but felt stuck in her sales job and certain her boss hated her, which left her feeling 'small, crappy and low'. After prodding her shortcut assumption with the questions above, she realized that her boss's occasional curtness was probably more to do with stress than a personal vendetta. Once our brains make shortcuts, they home in on corroborating evidence, screening out what doesn't fit our assumptions – especially if they sense potential threat. So Rachel screened out those times her boss was encouraging and supportive. Now she felt more able to approach her and ask for some coaching, and was delighted when she agreed.

Exercise: Spotting Shortcuts

The habitual, shortcut view you have of yourself and the world profoundly affects the way you lead your life. Start to spot your own shortcuts as you have already started to do with the 'shoulds'. When you notice them, you can unwind them to take a different path. A good place to start is by spotting the language you use. Notice when you say to others or yourself:

- '*I can't* . . .' What if you substituted 'I don't want to' for this? This way you have more power and choice. Or 'I find it hard to . . . ', which keeps the door to growth open.
- '*People* . . . /*Things* . . . /*I always*/*never* . . .' Grab that generalization and give it a shake. Go the long way round to make it specific. As Jan said to me one day, 'I am never very good at knowing what I want.' But when I asked, 'Is that always true?' she became more accurate. 'I find it hard without structure. When I have that and someone to talk with, I have lots of ideas.'

Stress increases the speed and number of shortcuts our brains make. Rachel was also worried about money. Her self-talk was peppered with absolutes like 'I can't', 'never' and 'always'. It's breathtakingly privileged to say lack of money doesn't matter. It does. We all need shelter, food and clothing. Our worry can cause secondary problems. Stress causes our shortcutting brains to equate our limited financial resources with having no choice or freedom. I know how stressed I am about everything when I am worried about how to pay my bills. When this happens, I tend to make short-term decisions and don't see longer-term opportunities. Lack of money is one thing, the fear and sense of absolute stuckness that it causes is another. If we can unhook one from the other, then – like Rachel – we can start to see windows of freedom and choice, even small ones, which help us take more control, for instance by making a financial plan, seeing what we can do for free, such as calling someone to discuss an opportunity or ask for help, or going for a walk to ease stress, and so look at things more positively.

Slow down, spot the shortcut and take an alternative route. It doesn't have to be 100 per cent right but can at least open out other possibilities.

3. Busyness

Humans are amazing. One of the many things we're amazing at is being able to adapt psychologically and physiologically to our environment. Psychologists call this *entrainment.** But the fast pace, endless tasks, multiple distractions and arrhythmic nature of our modern world

---

* Entrainment describes the way the body gradually syncs with either a biological or external rhythm. For instance, if you hear music with a fast beat or watch an exciting film, your breathing and heart rate will increase. It also works in the other direction; if you listen to relaxing music or are in a peaceful setting, your breathing and heart rate will slow.

speed us up and make it hard to focus on anything for long. Busyness isn't just a way of being but a badge of honour in our culture. You'll rest when you're dead. You're 'lazy' when you take a break or if you haven't done everything on your to-do list every day. And you'd better have lots of things to do – work, making social arrangements, travel, updating social media – if not, are you lazy or a loser? Yikes, even I'm starting to worry just writing that sentence. Of course we are really busy. The number of choices and decisions we have has expanded hugely within a generation, which is a very short amount of time in terms of human evolution. I don't believe my ancestors had the twenty-three items I seem to permanently have on my to-do list, no matter how many I tick off. But even in our so-called leisure time, we're still busy. When I am lying in bed, I am still on my phone. I struggle to switch off – and then because I don't, I find it even harder to do so.

We need to get back to our roots. A huge amount of evidence shows that when we are in a less frenetic environment we become more calm, creative and take a bigger perspective. We have to choose this, though. In our fast-paced, technologically driven world, taking some small actions to redress the balance with some grounding activities away from screens has a huge effect because of our entrainment capability. Pull yourself away to take a few minutes every day to sit in a park for instance, looking at the sky, trees and plants. Get into the practice of standing or sitting on earth, rather than rushing along on the tarmac checking your phone. Connection with nature has a profound biological and psychological effect. At the back of this book I have recommended some books with practices that will help. Even just setting aside time each day to switch your phone or at least your notifications off will start to make a huge difference. One of my clients used to do a ritual at 9 p.m. She would switch off her phone, wrap it in a lovely cloth, thank it for being so helpful throughout her day and put it in a carved wooden box, which she didn't open again until thirty minutes after she got out of bed the next day. Bless her, it was hard at first, but before long she loved it.

4. Rewards

We are motivated by two things – necessities, such as food and sleep, and rewards, which can be anything that increases pleasure or lowers pain. Your brain's reward centre lights up not just when you *experience* something that feels good but also when you *anticipate* it, sending signals to release the neurotransmitter dopamine, which motivates you to pursue it. Next time you feel the satisfaction of ticking unimportant tasks off your to-do list, or that buzz of receiving likes on social media, or the temptation to please your boss or a friend rather than tell them something difficult, your reward centre might be calling the shots.

Nowadays, besieged by so many ways to get easy rewards, we find it harder than ever to delay gratification. Yes, that's me on the sofa, phone in hand, looking up the ending of the film I am supposedly watching in order to relax. Every time I receive a reward (it was the ex-boyfriend who did it), the inner hunter-seeker wants more (who is the lead actress dating?), which is quite a distraction when I am trying to stay focused.

This isn't a bad thing in itself, and when we are trying to create a good new habit such as exercise, once we anticipate reward we'll be more motivated to put on our running shoes on a cold winter morning. However, our reward centre isn't great at waiting for the long-term benefits of exercise when there's the short-term pleasure of staying in bed, which is why we can fall off the wagon of our good intentions so often. It is fundamentally a crude system that seeks the quickest way to get a reward, and the architects of our modern consumer and techno-logical culture know this and exploit it without mercy.

In a very short period of time, smartphones in par-ticular have pulled our attention away from being present and aware to that tempting hunt for an instant, short-term reward. Studies suggest that merely the presence of a smartphone nearby reduces memory capacity, fluid intelligence and attention, and more research indicates that there's even a measurable effect when a phone is on silent mode compared to when it's switched off. Now-adays our attention drifts to our phones because we can't bear silence and stillness any more – states we need to be okay with so we can stop the world and reflect.

How about I admit I am not really invested in this film and do something more beneficial instead, like read, call a friend, exercise, make a nice meal, meditate or journal? Oh, but look, someone's liked my social media post. All day we are pummelled from outside by cognitive popcorn – as our culture bombards us with a blizzard of notifications, interruptions and distractions, and on the inside thoughts, desires and impulses burst from the hot pan of our minds. As a result, we are losing the ability to be still, focus and keep our eyes on the prize of the long-term reward.

5. Shoulds

You have already met these inner scripts. They don't just influence the big picture of what we do with our lives, they exert power over what we do with our days and hours. For example, one of the reasons Jan was constantly exhausted was because she kept accepting social invitations, despite the negative effects. She no longer even enjoyed the company of her old gang. But she accepted their invitations out of loyalty to their shared history and to an old self-image of being a girl-about-town. Our 'shoulds', charged up with habit-power, often shore up self-images that have passed their expiry date and activities that no longer serve us. While of course we want to be good friends (and to have fun), our own needs matter and change, and balancing this is important for those wanting to find their own path.

Where does this leave you? There is a battle raging for your attention on several fronts and, without care, you'll find it difficult to win. How would it feel to be able to tune into yourself, notice when the call to arms rings out and calmly step away from the battlefield into a deeper focus on yourself? What if, when you do, that wild, shy deer of your deeper, authentic Big I arrives and stays long enough for you to listen to it? I am going to suggest a couple of ways we can get our habits, shortcuts, busy-ness, short-term gratifications and 'shoulds' out of the driving seat of our lives, so that our wiser selves can take the wheel.

Cultivating Present Awareness

Put down this book and sit still for the next five minutes. Every time you have a thought or a desire to do something else, make a mark on a piece of paper. Then take a look when the time ends and you'll see the paw print of what Buddhists and mindfulness teachers call the 'monkey mind'.

Our minds generate thousands of thoughts a day, leaping from one to another like primates through trees. Having thoughts isn't an issue in itself; it's part of what the mind does. Our problem is that each thought can come with its own little hook or attachment, and we don't want to be carried away on them. When I sit down to do something that takes focus, I instantly think of something else to do – call a friend, check social media or make yet another cup of tea. It's as if the mind runs ahead and our Little I chases, hooked and overwhelmed.

Time for a tough truth. We can take a sabbatical once a week from our phones or go on a retreat, but we quickly return to our old habits. You can't stop the world happening around you, any more than you can completely stem the flow of thoughts and impulses within you. But here's the good news: if we create daily habits of present awareness – being present enough to notice when those hooks tug at us – we can open up enough space to choose what we want to engage with, when and how. Having a meditation or mindfulness practice can be incredibly useful for this, as brain-scanning technology shows. Personally, I find meditation helps me because I can better notice when my mind wanders off, and can return to awareness of what's going on in the present. When I meditate and focus on my breathing or the sensations of my body, I feel as if I am connecting to what's actually real, rather than the virtual reality of my thoughts about the past or worries about the future. In my everyday life, my practice gives me the benefit of knowing that I can access inner peace, not to escape the worries of my life but to better deal with them from a place of groundedness, and to have a sense of perspective. If you would like to start or develop your own practice, there are lots of great apps, websites and books that can help, and I recommend a few at the end of this book.

The even better news is that the simplest of mindfulness nudges practised regularly and embedded as habit into our daily lives can rewire us from reacting automatically to responding thoughtfully. Here's one of the best techniques I know.

Exercise: Here I Am

I used to meditate with a group. Once, after we ended a meditation, our teacher invited questions, and someone took her up.

'Right now, I feel so calm. But I know that if I open the door and see the bus, I'll start panicking I am going to miss it, and all my calm will vanish in a second. How do I stay in this bubble?'

'Mindfulness is not about creating a bubble of calmness,' the teacher wisely replied. 'It is simply to notice wherever you are at that moment. Try saying, "*Here I am* feeling rushed. *Here I am* running for the bus."'

We are not our thoughts and impulses. We are people *having* them, and with practice, we can mindfully detach from them and choose whether to follow or not. The part of you who can do this – who says, 'Here I am' – is the deeper, wiser self, less at the whim of our monkey minds. We want this part of ourselves to be in charge more.

Practise this simple reminder to shift into present awareness several times a day, for instance:

Here I am about to pick up my phone.

Here I am about to say yes to another commitment when my week already has little or no time for me.

Here I am about to do errands that can wait.

The mind doesn't work alone. We think, 'I am going to miss the bus!' and panic. We think, 'Here I am' and start to feel a little calmer. What's going on here? In Western culture, we tend to regard our bodies as brain taxis. However, the body and mind are not separate but intimately connected and integrated through our nervous systems. If your body is stressed, that will affect how you think and feel, and the thoughts we have affect our bodies in an instant – if you think you're going to miss a bus, for example. You can create more space and time for yourself by soothing the reactive stress patterns in your body-mind, working through your body to calm your mind. To tune in to the body-mind requires a trip back in time to understand what's happening, so you can spot it and take action.

How to Regulate Stress

Back in prehistoric times, two early human clans sit around on a plain. An unfamiliar creature approaches, and while one clan admires the sun glinting off its teeth, the other grabs its young and runs away. Not surprisingly, we are the descendants of the worriers. The stress we curse ourselves for in the modern world is a powerful evolutionary advantage. It's so sensitive that we not only react with fear to real and present threat but also to uncertainty and the unknown, and to what we imagine might happen. It's hardly surprising then that when we want to create a new act in our lives, not knowing what might happen if we step out of our comfort zones sends waves of anxiety crashing over us.

Actual or imagined threats aren't our only sources of stress. Because we are susceptible to the promise of reward, we are affected by *pleasure stress*. If someone offers you a pay rise, your heart will race and your focus narrow — the same effect as when your ancestors saw the predator. I have had more than one client thrown off the path to a life of greater meaning by the offer of a promotion in a role they didn't actually like.

Two truths I want you to know: one, not finding your own path can be stressful; two, finding your own path can be stressful. There is nothing wrong with stress; it's natural and normal, not shameful or a sign of weakness. We forget we're animals with iPhones. I don't believe we should aim for universal serenity, because we need a measure of stress to make things happen, and civil and human rights, for example, wouldn't progress without it. However, there's a distinction between the 'healthy stress' of positive motivation, the kind that has us bouncing out of bed in the morning, and 'toxic stress', which savages our ability to focus, solve problems, manage emotions, empathize, be kind to others and ourselves, collaborate, see the big picture, create and innovate, perceive reality as it is, have a growth mindset, and feel joyful – all the capacities we need to move from where we are to where we want to be. Our problem is that in our busy lives stress has become our default, and when it's default, it's toxic. This deeply affects our mental, physical, emotional and spiritual health. Eventually, it can bring us to a crisis, as Yasmin Khan told me,

'I was doing a very high-pressure job for many years, constantly run down and necking another coffee or painkillers to get through. Eventually, I became very ill, which was hugely challenging because my whole identity was about being able to cope. I mean, who has a nervous breakdown?'

We don't even notice when stress becomes our norm, so recognizing the signs helps us catch it quickly *before* we hit the wall at a hundred miles an hour like Yasmin.

Notice Your Stress Reactions

When you understand more about what happens to you when you get stressed, you can spot your own stress patterns and take action. Right now, you're quietly reading this book, or listening to it on audio. Imagine that, out of the blue, someone throws a ball at you. You'd feel startled. Just imagining it might have given you a small tingle. The sympathetic branch of your autonomic nervous system almost instantly triggers, like an accelerator in a car, providing you with adrenaline-fuelled energy so that you can survive danger. Now imagine that someone places a thick bundle of cash in front of you, or that the person you fancy just sat down in front of you or, dare I say it, just take a glance at your phone. The sympathetic branch may kick up again with pleasure stress to help you gain something you want. How long did it take you to get back to this book once I mentioned your phone? Evidence suggests that just thinking about it will start to affect your concentration. Welcome back.

Whether triggered by danger or desire, when our bodies flood with adrenaline – that heart-clenching, stomach-churning, muscle-tightening sensation – you have an opportunity to notice it: 'Here I am feeling triggered.' But it happens so fast we might not catch it. In case we miss it, we have a second chance by noticing the thoughts and behaviours that typically follow. Broadly speaking, in the case of danger, when we are vulnerable, we have five possible stress reaction patterns – all fine evolutionary survival strategies that well served our ancestors, and many other animals. They are useful for us to know because, one, by spotting our patterns we notice we're triggered, and, two, we can identify our own personal patterns, reflect on how useful they are and whether we might want to change them. When someone throws a ball at you, your stress reactions can reduce your physical vulnerability, but – and this is important to understand – you also have typical stress reaction patterns when you feel *emotionally* vulnerable. What if this person hurt you with words rather than a ball? Here are the five stress reaction patterns:

Fight: You might angrily confront the person: 'Hey, what the hell? Why would you do that, you git?' Do you tend to go on the attack when someone says or does something that triggers your vulnerability?

Flight: You might leap up to get out of the line of the ball. Great, you live to see another day. But would you then avoid a potential confrontation with the person who threw it by looking at your phone, cracking a joke or changing the subject, even if you felt shocked? Would your pattern be to pretend it didn't matter? Then you're in flight, rather than asserting boundaries or your own needs.

Freeze: Would you tense like a rabbit in the headlights, unable to move, overwhelmed? If I feel emotionally vulnerable, for instance, when I receive unexpected bad news, or when someone close to me is expressing powerful emotions – or I need to – I often have this reaction. I have a similar reaction when a ball comes at me, which is why I am rubbish at tennis.

Fold: Would you sigh and collapse on the inside, thinking something like, 'This always happens to me'?

Fawn: Would you immediately try to avoid any conflict and cover up how stressed and vulnerable you feel by trying to please the git who threw the ball at you or who said something harsh?

What do you recognize in yourself? Once you know your tendencies, you'll be better able to spot when you are stressed. Again, there's no shame, it's normal, so don't sharpen any of this into a stick to jab yourself with; it's just helpful to be more aware so you can take action to help.

Journal Questions

Write about moments of stress in your journal, note what happens and reflect:

- What is/are my typical stress reaction/s?
- Are they useful, or not?
- Do I want to change them?
- What would be more useful?

How do we start to have a little more control and regain our composure quickly once triggered, whether by physical or emotional vulnerability, perceived danger or

70

the promise of pleasure – especially the quick-hit kind that our brain's reward centres respond to so powerfully? When we want to find our own paths, developing our ability to notice and regulate our stress is invaluable when we are pushed by those 'shoulds', pulled by those distractions, and overwhelmed with fear at the unknown over the threshold before us. We have another branch of our autonomic nervous system, the parasympathetic one, which acts like a brake, allowing us to slow down so we can feel more in control and make conscious choices for ourselves. We can't help feeling triggered at times, so it is unrealistic for any of us to imagine we could be calm all the time. However, we can do something to find the brake as soon as we notice.

Manage Your Stress

I use techniques called centering that calm us by releasing key points in our bodies that activate when we are triggered by perceived or actual threat or pleasure. When we are stressed, our muscles tense and contract, and our perception and awareness narrow to focus on the source of the threat or the quickest way to escape. (Remember the predator heading towards our ancestors?) When we centre, we mindfully ease these physical reactions, signalling to the brain that it's okay, which then takes its foot off the gas. Centering isn't a shortcut to zen calm (although all my clients instantly feel the results, with some even reporting they feel as if they had done an hour of yoga in one minute), but when you can find the brake for unhelpful automatic reactivity, you create the space to choose consciously.

I was taught the two following techniques on my training with the Embodied Facilitator Course by the estimable Paul Linden. My clients find both supremely useful whether they are being bombarded with cognitive popcorn from within, or those millions of possible distractions and temptations from without, or when they feel overwhelmed at the prospect of focusing on what they want to do with their lives. We all have the ability to rewire our brains to a certain extent with regular practice. Practising centering several times a day will help rewire your stress reactions more effectively and for longer than a fortnight on a beach. The trick is remembering to do it. However, once you build the habit, it will come more easily, quickly and automatically.

Practice: Centering

1. Soften your belly. Ask yourself, 'Could my belly be at least 10 per cent more relaxed?'
2. Notice what that feels like. You may become aware of sensations in your lower back and pelvis as your core releases.
3. Keep that softness in your belly, and release tension in your jaw. Ask yourself if your jaw could be 10 per cent more relaxed.
4. As I mentioned, when you are stressed, your focus narrows to the perceived source of threat or reward. Expanding your perception will help shift you to a more relaxed inner state. With that softness in your belly and jaw, follow with one

of these techniques. With practice, you'll discover which works for you:

- Imagine that you are a lightbulb, with light radiating in all directions around you, or that you are expanding into the space all around you.
- Think of someone or something that makes you smile, or visualize your heart shining out.
- Gently open your arms wide to the furthest point where you can still see both thumbs in your peripheral vision, whilst keeping your head and eyes facing front. Drop your arms and maintain this focus.

Practise at least three times a day initially, for instance when waiting for the kettle to boil, before or during a meeting or – when you have practised enough – in a conversation with someone, while still keeping attention on them. Note down how you feel afterwards in your journal to remind you in case you forget later, and to motivate you to keep going. As you practise and become more familiar with centering, simplify by saying:

Belly
Jaw
Shine or expand

The beauty is that with practice, once you notice you are stressed, you can do this without anyone else noticing.

I like to take this one step further so clients can check

in with what they need, using the beautiful practice below. Try it and see what you feel.

Practice: Six Directions Breathing

This is another of Paul Linden's centering techniques, and one of my other teachers, Francis Briers, suggested the questions at the end. In this practice, you exhale in different directions through your body, as if aiming your breath. It works because by practising intending to open your body outward in a number of directions, you develop the habit of keeping open and balanced, no matter what stress you encounter. The first time you try this, I recommend you breathe several times in each direction. Once you have practised this, you can then try one breath in each direction in a cycle of seven breaths, and you can also experiment with how far you can focus your breath and notice what happens as you aim it further out.

1. Sit upright in a chair with your feet flat on the floor, or if you prefer being on the floor, sit with your legs crossed, one ankle in front on the other with both on the floor to give you stability, or kneel with your heels under your tailbone. If you are sitting in a chair or cross-legged on the floor, it helps to place a large rolled towel under your tailbone at the base of your spine. Your sit bones should stay on the chair or floor. This supports you so you feel freer and taller because

you don't need as much tension and energy to keep yourself upright.

2. Close your eyes. Relax your belly and jaw, as in the previous centering practice. Breathe in, imagining that you are drawing in your breath from a point below your navel.

3. Then exhale through your mouth, relaxing your mouth and throat.

4. As you exhale, imagine that you are gently blowing the air down your spinal column, out of the bottom of it, to a spot six or eight inches below you. Don't just think about this or picture it in your mind but actually feel it in your body, sensing the lower part of your spine and the direction of flow, if possible. It might take a few tries, especially if this is your first time, so practise for half a dozen breaths. Notice how it feels to you today. One day might feel strong, another less so. There's no right or wrong; you're just noticing, and this attention is great.

5. Breathe in again, then, as you exhale gently through your mouth, feel that you are exhaling up your spinal column, out of the top of your head, to a spot six or eight inches above you. Repeat six times if you need.

6. Breathe in again and, as you exhale, feel as if you are pushing your breath out of your left side to a spot about six inches away. Repeat as before. Then change direction to your right side.

7. Inhale, and with your next exhalation, feel that you are pushing your breath out into the space

behind you, as if your back opens to let it out. Again, do this six times until you feel you have got the hang of it. Repeat for the front.

8. Finally, take a few breaths feeling you are exhaling in all six directions at once. Notice how you feel.

9. You can stop here, if you wish, but to add another layer, ask yourself the following question in each direction, and notice what you sense in your body. Don't worry if nothing is clear; you're just shaking the tree.

> *Down* – 'How grounded do I feel?'
> *Up* – 'How inspired, creative and/or confident do I feel?'
> *Left* – 'Am I listening, receiving and being? Am I connecting with people?'
> *Right* – 'Am I taking action and doing?'
> *Behind* – 'Who and what has my back?' These can be people, those who came before you, and/or your own story.
> *Front* – 'Do I feel aligned with how I am showing up in the world?'

These questions aren't fixed, and with practice you may create your own. I do this every day to check in with myself and what I might need. Sometimes I notice that I sense a weakness on the 'down' breath. Am I a bit too much in my head, being tossed around by torrents of thoughts? Maybe I need to slow down, ground myself and focus on one practical step at a time. Other times, I sense that pushing my breath out towards left or right feels like curling wisps of smoke, rather than a focused powerful flow, which might suggest that I haven't been connecting with others recently, going it alone in isolation. Time to reach out and connect. I also practise Six Directions Breathing whenever I feel anxious, before delivering a talk or a session with a client to shake off some of the stress that builds up and to feel more spacious and calm.

Once you have started to take steps to switch off automatic with mindful awareness and stress regulation, you can build in the time and space you need to find your own path. You are ready to choose the bigger yes that is going to help push back against the small yeses with which we automatically and mindlessly react to our monkey minds and the world. It's like having a bouncer between the demands and distractions, and the VIP area of your life.

Your Bigger Yes

Like many of you, I can be a small-yes person: yes to scrolling the web when I wake up or squeezing another client into an already full day. Now I consider my bigger yes. When I say no to scrolling, I am saying a bigger yes to feeling clear-headed and doing something that feels better – like exercise or getting outside. When I say no to a client, I am saying a bigger yes to needed rest. When Jan now says no to a friend, she is saying yes to time to focus on herself. When Rachel says no to spending money on something she doesn't need, she is saying yes to building up her savings, and having less anxiety and more confidence that she can create a new life.

Practice: Your Bigger Yes

1. Look again at your awareness diary from the start of this chapter.
2. Identify what you would like to say no to – including tasks, invitations and habits. Ask of each, does this enlarge or diminish me? If the latter, can you say no? If not, how can you limit it?
3. Write down the bigger yes behind those nos.
4. Cancel or stop as many nos as you can.
5. Now when an invitation or habit comes up, pause with 'Here I am' and centre before you follow through. Imagine if you said no, what your bigger yes would be. If it's a big yes already, great. If not, no.

These practices of mindfulness and stress regulation aren't just tools to help you find your own path, they are the foundation of it. You have what you need to begin moving from being lost in the woods. Now you are ready to cultivate your relationship with the Big I to find your own path and make it a meaningful one. In the next chapter, you're going to ask some Big I questions to tease it out and start one of the most important conversations of your life.

3. Start the Conversation

If you ceased reacting to everything around you, who would you be? This chapter is about starting a conversation with our Big I – that inner, deeper self that gets crowded out by the noise in our lives. Like meeting that deer in the woods, you can only connect once you quieten distractions and mind, switch off autopilot, and create space for yourself. The previous chapter aimed to help you do that; this one is about what you can do once you have, with some of my favourite self-reflection exercises to help you. Self-reflection builds self-awareness, which you can't find your own path without – and your Big I holds lots of possible clues. Take some time for each set of questions, write your responses in your journal, and welcome in what you discover. Read it back afterwards and highlight the words and phrases that resonate with you. Each one is a seed. You may not yet know what's going to grow, but don't worry about that. Don't push things faster than they need to go right now. This is where you start exploring the questions that will help you find your own path. You're going to take your responses and fashion them into a compass that will help guide your way in the next chapter.

Journalling is one of the best ways to coax the Big I out of hiding. Writing time is thinking time. We start to slow down and listen to ourselves. Personally, I often find journalling hard. With free writing, I can turn out pages of blah. A bit of structure helps to lay the foundations of self-knowledge upon which we can build our path. These four writing exercises help you do some of that groundwork and start the Big I conversation. You don't have to do all of them, and I wouldn't recommend you try them all in one day. Each one can bring up a lot, so it's a good idea to let what comes up sink in and integrate into your conscious awareness. I recommend you set aside some time, about thirty minutes to an hour at one time. Everything you discover now will come in useful as you go forward, so don't see these exercises as something you write down and then forget about. Get into the practice of rereading your journal – it's a rich resource.

With these writing prompts, you become a time traveller moving back along your timeline to reconnect with what's important to you and forward to reap energy from the vision of the future you want. Pick up your journal and get into your time machine; you're going beyond the Little I of your daily habits, busyness, shortcuts, rewards and 'shoulds'. It's time to meet your Big I.

1. Remembering and Retrieving

As you stand lost in the woods, with the potential of a rich and rewarding path of your own ahead, you don't need to reinvent yourself completely so much as remember yourself anew. As you seek your own path, you don't go forward with empty hands, you carry something essential of yourself. To be an adult, you gave up being a child, but in the process you may have left behind something precious that you need to retrieve now.

Exercise: Remember Who You Are

Remember when you were a small child, no more than seven years old. Think of something you loved to do or be, something which expressed your essential nature.

Use these prompts to help you. If one doesn't work for you, then don't worry, move on to another or create your own. Write down your responses.

- First, imagine you are that child again. What would you say? 'I feel . . . I love . . . I need . . .'

Now, from where you are today, reflect on these prompts:

- What do you want to give this child?
- What would you like to do and be with them?
- How would you take care of them and encourage them to grow?
- Now imagine that child speaks back to you. What do they want you to know that you have forgotten?

As a child, I loved playing in nature for hours. I also loved to dance, read and write stories. I also cared about others naturally. My mother tells me I used to soothe other infants in my foster home when they were distressed by reaching out my little hand and patting them. Lots of seeds there.

As you reconnect with yourself as a child, you may also recall gifts you received in childhood. Ali agreed to tell her story for this book, and started with her own early life, growing up in a working-class household. Those roots gave her something special, which she carries throughout her life and work.

'My dad died when I was thirteen, leaving my mum with five children and my nana in a housing estate and with very little money. And my mother was magnificent because out of those conditions grew five company directors, serial entrepreneurs – not just to create income but for purpose, meaning and contribution. And that was something she planted in our lives for each of us.'

She glows with positivity as she recalls those early years. She understands that the values of love, care, self-determination and responsibility were gifts, and she and her siblings live by them every day.

2. Connect with Your Story

We forget how far we've come. The seeds for your own path are already in your life.

Exercise: Your Story

In whichever way suits you, create a timeline of your life. Some people like to draw a simple line from birth to the present moment; others draw a map of a road or river running through a landscape.

Once you have done this, sit back and take a look. Identify moments where you made a positive choice — perhaps a job or project you took or left, a relationship you began or ended, a friend you made, somewhere you chose to live, somewhere you chose to go or something you did with your time.

Note down what guided you to make that choice. What was important to you at that point?

3. Say Hello to Your Deeper Self
Exercise: What's Important Now?

Use some or all of the questions below as journalling prompts. The first time you do it, I recommend you reflect on the past twelve months, but this is a great quarterly or monthly practice. It's not an exam, so don't feel you have to answer all the questions. Perhaps spend some time with those that appeal right now.

Looking Back

- When I look back over this time period, what am I most grateful for?
- What am I most proud of?
- What did I learn?
- How have I been open-minded and open-hearted?
- When have I felt most alive? What was important about that?

- How was I compassionate to myself and to others?
- What were my greatest challenges? How did I handle them? How do I feel about how I faced them?
- What was out of my control?
- What was in my control, and what did I choose to be and do? What was important about that?
- What was my greatest contribution?
- Who has inspired me? Why?
- What was the best decision I made? Why?
- What was the biggest risk I took?
- What do I want to credit myself for?
- What do I wish I had done more of?
- What do I wish I had done less of?
- When did I feel most connected to myself?
- What was the kindest service I performed?
- What was the kindest service I received?
- What was the best way I used my time?

Now

- At this point in my life, what is most important to me?
- If I could choose one thing to be known for, what would it be?
- Where am I feeling stuck?
- Where is it time to let go?

- What do I commit to now? Why is that important?
- What first small step could I realistically take now that would make the biggest and most positive difference?
- Regardless of what other changes I might make, what am I certain I want to keep?

Looking Forward

- How do I want to feel this time next year?
- What will I take from this time as best practice for the rest of my life?

We'll delve more deeply into your future with the next set of questions.

4. Imagine Your Future Self

Separation from your old life is easier when you have a guiding image of your future. A list is not going to cut it. What you want is a *vision* – a picture that will inspire you. When I ask people what they want, they often falter or come up with something inauthentic. But deep inside you there is a hidden image. You just need to ask the right questions to release it – and they may surprise you.

Exercise: Your Future Self

1. Stand in a space where you can take about ten steps ahead. Where you stand represents this moment, and each step forward represents six months in the future. If your movement is restricted, place objects in a line in front of you on a table, each object representing six months in the future. So one step or the first object is six months from now, the next is six months on from that, and so on.

2. Move along this timeline with your feet or eyes until you reach a sweet spot – the point at which you would like to be following your own path. Don't rush, and don't overthink. When you slow down, you'll be more able to tap into what your body feels like. Use the Goldilocks principle: one place might feel too cold and remote, another too hot and pressurized. Does one step feel too soon? Three feel too far in the future? As always, there's no right or wrong. Start by asking, 'When would I like to be on my own path?' and once you find a spot, ask, 'When would be most realistic?' If there's a difference, choose 'realistic' to ease the pressure on yourself.

3. Imagining yourself at this point in your future, ask yourself the following questions and note any answers:
   - What are you wearing on your feet?
   - What about your clothes?

- What surface are you standing on?
- Are you inside a room? What do the walls and windows look like? What's the size and feel of the room? What's in it?
- If you are outside, what are the details of your environment? What can you feel under your feet and against your skin? What can you smell?
- Are you alone? What are you doing? Why?
- Are you with other people or beings? How many? Why do they want to be with you? What are you doing together, and why?
- How do you feel? It's vital to log a felt sense of this experience.
- Note down anything else you notice in your imagination.

4. Create an 'anchor' to help capture this. It can be an object, a piece of music or video, a single image or a mood board, with a collage of images. Be discerning with images from magazines or social media posts, as they are masters at parading images of what we *should* want. When I imagined becoming a life coach, I searched online and found lots of images of women in yoga poses on white sandy beaches. But this didn't feel authentic, as my vision of my future self is in deep connection with other people and definitely isn't wearing a bikini.

The journey to find your own path doesn't start with moving out but moving in to connect with your Big I.

You are digging deep into those layers, reaping valuable information and messages from yourself to yourself. In the next chapter, you'll do more digging, building on your responses to these exercises to unearth the elements of the compass that will guide you.

4. Build Your Compass

With all the demands of everyday life, it's easy to get lost and lose track of your own unique sense of self and what really matters to you. We can vaguely long for a more meaningful life, but what would that actually look like? From where we are in the woods, we might catch a glimpse of a ridge that looks lovely, but the river valley also beckons, and there's much more we can't see from here. How would you know where you want to go, and how would you get there? Which part of yourself decides – Little I, caught up in the 'shoulds', short-term rewards and habits of day-to-day life, or Big I, with all that rich potential inside? Small wonder it's easier to follow a predetermined road – and most of them are clearly marked on your old map of life. You have already started to shake free the seeds of what's important to you; now you're going to continue the conversation to fashion a guidance system – your own personal compass or GPS – so you can find your own path.

Congratulations on starting to separate from old scripts that no longer serve you and making time and space for your Big I. Now you are beginning the transition from the life that you know into the unknown. To find a new path, you first need a compass to keep you aligned with that authentic Big I self, so you know which direction follows your North Star. If you plot a course out of your current life without one, you risk following a path not your own or getting lost again. Your North Star is your authentic *values-in-action* — what's important to you, the beliefs or principles that motivate and guide your choices and actions from within, rather than those 'shoulds', scripts, habits and automatic reactions we encountered in Chapters One and Two. When you live your life aligned with your values, you feel more motivated and energized, and you attract people and opportunities that share them. That's exactly how you want to feel on your path. This chapter will help you identify your values, keep yourself aligned with them and put them into action, so you can start walking it.

Set Your Compass

I'd like to share with you the North Star that guides my own path. My values-in-action are Love & Connection, Growth & Learning, Service, Exploration & Creativity. Whenever I think about a new project, where and how I want to live, and with whom I want to spend my time, I check my compass and ask, 'How would this choice align with my values?' It keeps me on my path when the 'shoulds' and the 'always have dones' pound upon my door. If a direction or choice doesn't align with my values, it's not going to be the path I want.

For instance, I once worked in an environment in which we rarely tried anything new without going through layers of management. I sat behind a desk all day and hardly talked to anyone. As a result, I felt constrained and inauthentic because my work was misaligned with my values. I wanted to connect deeply with people, help them come up with ideas, put them into action, see how they turned out, and learn from that. I do that as a coach, facilitator and writer, and my values don't only guide my career. I am interested in people and their journeys, excited by nature and ideas. I love to learn and give myself opportunities to do that, even if it's reading an article, listening to a podcast or watching a documentary or talk. I value compassion, empathy, kindness, humility, courage and growth, and my friends share this. When I started working with a coach, uncovering my own values was my first step, and when I later trained as a coach with the Co-Active Training Institute, I learned how to help people discover theirs. I can't emphasize enough how vital your values are to finding and walking your own path.

By now you may be asking yourself, How do I clarify my own values-in-action? Great question! You are going to build on your responses to the exercises in the previous chapter to help you to do that shortly. But first, I want to get clear on what I mean by a value, because there are some common traps you need to steer clear of.

Don't Confuse an Interest or Strength with a Value

A value is not an interest like nature or travel. Confusing them can cause problems. For instance, dating sites match people based on shared interests, which is not a bad start.

However, you can share interests without always sharing values, which are more helpful in forming successful long-term relationships. If, say, I was matched with someone who also likes walking, and arrived on our date to find the other person ready to race me up the nearest hill because they value Competition and Winning, my heart would sink (shortly before my lungs collapsed). Although we share the same interest, our values may be misaligned. I value Exploration and Connection, and delight in hidden paths and details, and sharing the beauty of the discovery with someone. Needless to say, they might not enjoy dating me either. Wandering off to look at a tree, or pausing to take in the view or have a chat, I would only slow them down.

When we dig deeper into what is important about our interests, we'll discover our values. The exercise later will help you do this.

Similarly, although you can feel crushed if you aren't expressing your strengths, you need to have some discernment here. A strength isn't always a North Star to set your compass to. I have some strengths as an editor – the ability to make connections, to see patterns, to understand ideas, and to spot problems and fuzzy thinking. Much of the energy for this came from my underlying value of Learning – and years of practice and training have made me a fine intellectual assassin. But if I had to sit poring over manuscripts every day, I would quickly feel demotivated. Even though I never want to stop learning, reading manuscripts on my own isn't the best way for me to live a life of Connection. Some strengths energize you – often because they also are an expression of a value. But other strengths can de-energize you, even though you're good at them. Would living your life by a strength alone be enough to motivate you to get out of bed in the morning? If you know your strengths, ask where the energy and commitment to build them came from. Is there an underlying value that would energize you?

Set Your Compass by Your Intrinsic Values

Don't imagine that you're searching for values that somehow make you a 'worthy' person, or that 'compassion' is better than 'ambition', or vice versa. A value is not good or bad – if you find yourself judging or ashamed of any of them, that's the echo of a script. What is important is that they are *your* values. Many of the 'shoulds' in your life are often powered by *extrinsic* values – external to you, often absorbed from culture or family. Although not bad or wrong, extrinsic values are not authentic, and to live your life by them can leave you feeling de-energized and unfulfilled, even if there are other benefits. Set your compass to *intrinsic* values – ones that are authentically yours.

For example, my client Maria was a woman in her fifties who realized that although her work as a college professor aligned with extrinsic values of Achievement and Prestige – which were a big deal as she was among the first generation from her working-class immigrant family to get a degree – she felt empty, heavy and down.

'It's hard to go in every day, because you don't feel like you're the person for the job. It feels inauthentic, and I felt ashamed because I didn't really care any more about the work that I was doing.'

When you set your compass to intrinsic values, you are more likely to feel energized, motivated over the long term, engaged, purposeful and that your life aligns with who you are on the inside. When she decided to support a community radio station get back up and running on a hurricane-devastated island, Maria started to feel alive and inspired again because what she was doing aligned with her intrinsic values of Helping Others, Civic Engagement and Community. As she described the project, her face lit up. Now in her new career as a therapist, she brings these values into action by offering pricing options that are accessible for other women in her community. The exercise coming up is going to uncover your intrinsic values, and you'll know they are authentic by feeling the way Maria did – lit from the inside.

Be Clear and Nuanced About What Your Values Mean

Here's something else you need to watch out for. The same word used to describe a value can take on different flavours for different people. As an example, let's listen in again to two people on a date. One says that they value honesty and the other nods enthusiastically, hopeful they may have met their match. However, by 'honesty', one person means they will be monogamous. The other won't, but will be honest about it. In dating and in life, be clear on what you mean by the words or phrases you use to describe what's important to you. You'll discover more about the nuances of your values by living them, and I'll offer suggestions for how to do this after the exercise.

Make Sure Your Values Are Up to Date

Values change over time. One of the reasons you are feeling lost may be that you are leading your life according to values that do not resonate so strongly with you as they once did.

For instance, until he reached his threshold, Pratam, a client of mine, had a core value of Saying Yes to new experience. And of course, his life was rich, varied and full of excitement. Now in his mid-thirties, he no longer wanted to sacrifice solitude and the rest he needed to prioritize his emerging value of Creativity. Time to reset the compass.

If you partner up, become parents, face adversity and struggles, as you age, as your own parents age and die, and as our collective values move from consumption to responsibility, happiness to meaning, living for the moment to living in a way that reduces our footprint on the planet and increases positive impact, you may find your values shift. Checking your North Star and resetting your compass every few years ensures you are aligning your life with your values *now*, not with some out-of-date version of yourself and what used to leave you feeling fulfilled.

Look for Your Values-in-action rather than Aspirational Values

We're nearly ready to identify your values-in-action. But just before we do, I want to warn you not to make the mistake many people do. You'll notice I have included a list of examples of values. You wouldn't be the first person to feel tempted to sneak a peek and tick off the ones that appeal. Resist the temptation. There are many values to which we might *aspire*, many that sound great, many we might like to say are our guiding star, and many we might enjoy, but are they the ones we should actually live by? You may also find that you can tick off many, but which would be your priority – your *core* values?

If I look at the list, I would be tempted myself.

- I have Prudence with money, but this is a learned behaviour that – while important and helpful – doesn't exactly get me out of bed in the morning with a spring in my step and a sense of purpose.
- Although I enjoy Spontaneity, if I set my compass to that, I would feel out of control, and it certainly wouldn't be as important as Love & Connection or Growth. I can sacrifice a bit of spontaneity if I can align with them.
- Risk-taking sounds sexy. Given a choice, I'd like the world to see me as a risk-taker rather than someone who isn't. Our culture loves risk-takers, and if you don't believe me, take a look at the people who become its stars – entrepreneurs, sportspeople and social media celebrities who put their finances and bodies on the line. But

risk-taking is not something that guides my choices for its own sake. Sure, I have taken risks in my life, but in the service of my core values of Love & Connection, Growth & Learning, Service, Exploration and Creativity. If Risk-taking is a core value-in-action for you, then great, but remind me never to get in a car when you're driving or take your investment advice.

Let's start not with the list but with your life. This powerful exercise uses your responses to the questions from the previous chapter to help you discover your values. By becoming curious about your experiences, you can hear your life tell you your values, rather than you telling your life what they are.

Exercise: Your Values-in-action

Start with your own experiences. Lean in and listen to them with curiosity, and let them speak back to you. It's like meeting yourself anew, your best self, the self you want to be more often in your life from now on.

1. Take up your journal and read your answers to the questions from the previous chapter. Pay attention to the responses that excite you, especially to the following questions:
   • What did you love doing when you were a child, from the exercise Remember Who You Are?

- What were the positive choices in your life and what guided you to choose what you did, from the Your Story exercise?
- In the What's Important Now? questions, when you looked back over the last twelve months, which were the questions that really lit you up when you wrote your response? It might be what you were most proud of, your greatest contribution, when you felt most connected to yourself or what you would choose to be known for. Or it could be any others that you felt excited and energized writing about.
- What is it that excites you in your Future Self vision?

2. Once you have selected the responses that energize you, ask, 'What's important about this for me?' if you haven't already, to uncover your values. For instance, when you were a child, did you love Adventure? In your story, was there a moment when you took on a Challenge and had a meaningful sense of Achievement when you aced it? If you felt energized in the last year when you were with friends, was it because you were Making a Contribution in some way? Is it because you have a great sense of Trust with them? When you see yourself in the future, do you feel excited by the Freedom you have? Notice what happens in your body. When you hit a value, it's like striking gold. You'll feel a big

'yes'. If you feel uncertain, ask yourself this question: if you had to give up living this value, would you do it, even if you were offered other things you want? I know that for me, if I could never show Compassion to people (one of my core values within Love & Connection), then no thanks.

3. Write down a list of the values you uncover. This is where the list can help you to find the words, but feel free to come up with your own. You don't have to have individual words. A friend encapsulates all his values-in-action with the phrase 'like a gentleman'.

4. Prioritize your list into three to six core values to make it easier to remember. You can compound them. For instance, to me, my value of Growth & Learning includes Courage, and Love & Connection encompasses Kindness. You don't have to do this immediately, you can leave them, do some of the practices around putting your values into action below, and then come back when you have more clarity.

5. Put your value words where you can see them every day, for instance pinned up somewhere or on a screensaver until you feel familiar with them. You can also remind yourself of them with an object or picture.

Here is that list.

Abundance	Excellence	Professionalism
Accomplishment	Fairness	Progress
Achievement	Freedom	Prudence
Adventure	Growth	Purpose
Altruism	Harmony	Raising the bar
Ambition	Heart-led	Reciprocity
Appreciation	Home	Risk-taking
Authenticity	Honesty	Security
Balance	Humour	Self-expression
Beauty	Independence	Self-respect
Being the best	Influence	Service
Boldness	Integrity	Simplicity
Challenge	Intimacy	Spirituality
Compassion	Kindness	Spontaneity
Connection	Knowledge	Stability
Control	Leadership	Stewardship
Courage	Learning	Teaching
Creativity	Legacy	Teamwork
Curiosity	Loyalty	Tolerance
Democracy	Making a difference	Tradition
Dependability	Participation	Trust
Discipline	Perseverance	Truth
Discovery	Playfulness	Usefulness
Diversity	Power	Vision
Effectiveness	Precision	Wealth
Ethics	Productivity	Well-roundedness

Put Your Values into Action

Knowing your values is one thing but this won't instantly make your life more meaningful. There's a lot of evidence that putting them into action does, though, and it will also help clarify them. In psychological studies, the more people felt their lives were congruent or aligned with their values, the greater meaning they reported. Set your compass to your values, so that what you do, who you are and how you show up in the world are in alignment with them. Take it from Alana, a woman who – after a life-changing experience you'll hear more about in the next chapter – knows the benefits of living a life aligned with values.

'You need to know who you are. You need to know why you're there, and what matters to you when the slings and arrows push you around. You need ballast within. That's what gives you power. Good power.'

I earlier mentioned that it's important to put your values into action because you'll attract people and see possibilities that share those values and so offer ways you can live authentically. Maria discovered that being lit up with her values when she supported the island community radio station made people trust her and offer her opportunities:

'Because I was authentic, people would say, "Oh, sure, I'll help you, let me connect you to this person," and they'd take risks on my behalf. The director of the museum took me into his school. I didn't even speak the language fluently. It was a big thing for him to trust me, but he told me he realized I believed in what I was doing and genuinely wanted to help.'

If you like what you hear and long for some of Alana's sense of self and Maria's opportunities, then here are some ideas to put your values into action.

1. Practice: Use Your Compass

Once you have clarified your values, take some time to journal using the following prompts to check your compass. I recommend doing this every week or month.

- How am I living my values?
- How am I not living my values?

When you need to make a decision, use your values as a guide. Live them not just in *what* you do but in *how* you do it. Can you act in alignment with your values? Can you be who you are in essence?

Notice also when you feel frustrated or listless. This is a great opportunity to check your compass, as it could mean there's a value not being prioritized or observed. It's a great moment to identify what this might be, rather than looking for someone or something to blame. Remember when I was frustrated working alone behind a desk? Nothing was wrong with that, but because I value Connection I felt discontent. Once I knew that, I could start to change things. Sometimes you don't have to change job; clients of mine have asked for different responsibilities, managers or working hours, less isolation – or more – to align their work more closely with their values.

2. Practice: Set an Intention

I have a little jar containing my values written down on pieces of paper. When I am feeling a little stuck, lost or de-energized, I pick one of the pieces of paper from the jar at the start of my day, and use the value written there as my word for the day, using it as my guide. I recommend you try this yourself – it never fails to put a bit of zing, clarity, focus and meaning into what I do that day. You can do something in particular, such as volunteering, exploring options for a course to take or planning to meet up with friends, or you can bring that value to *how* you do something you already have planned. For instance, if you pick Appreciation, you could start a meeting by letting people know you value them, or end a call with family or friends the same way. Write in your journal what happens as a consequence and how you felt. Keep it up and soon living your values will be second nature – and that is your path. You can take even bigger steps by setting goals.

3. Exercise: Set Value-based Goals

Want to know the biggest mistake people make when they set goals? They start with the goal. If you are going to make sure you are in alignment with your values, the trick is to start with them, not with the goal itself. That way you know you are walking your own path, rather than living a 'should' or a script. Here's a way to do that.

1. Take a page in your journal and draw three columns. Write down a value that you want to bring more into your life in the first column. You can add more values on rows below, but don't work on more than four at any one time because you'll be overwhelmed.

2. In the next column, write at least one appealing way you might put that value into action. Your ideas don't have to be big or grand, but it does help to use the following guidelines:

   - What would this look like in action? Be clear, not vague. For instance, a few years ago, I wanted to prioritize my values of Creativity and Service by writing some workshops. I also wanted to have more Connection in my life, and decided to see friends more.

   - Be realistic. Although I might be able to envision a full suite of workshops, given the amount of work involved, it was more realistic to start with one. Seeing friends every day would be too exhausting.

   - Don't do something for the sake of it or because there's a 'should'. Will this help move your life in the meaningful direction you want?

   - How would you know you'd achieved it? I would have written and led one workshop, and seen friends twice a week, I decided.

   - Set a deadline or time to review. Initially, keep the longest deadline at a year maximum, which is what I did for writing workshops. Or you can keep it shorter, as I did for seeing friends. I decided to review after a month and see how I was feeling.

3. In the last column, write your first step. Get momentum going. Keep this small and something you can make a start on that week. 'Set aside an hour and brainstorm some possible topics' and 'Draw up a list of people with whom I'd like to spend more time' were good first steps for me.

4. After you have done this, take a fresh page in your journal. Draw a column down the left side and note in it your value goals, for instance, as I did, Creativity and below that Connection. Across the top mark weekly dates for a check-in. Use more pages as you go along. Each week, mark what you did to move forward, no matter how small the steps. Consistency matters when you are finding your own path, but if you don't manage one week (or more!), reset and continue when you can.

You wouldn't be the first person who finds it challenging to prioritize putting your values into action, especially because of our habits, shortcuts, busyness, short-term reward hunts and 'shoulds' – as we discovered in Chapter Two. Because of this, I am going to finish this chapter by giving you a new and useful way of creating a to-do list to make sure you have something to write every week in your journal. This new Values-led To-do List has been a game changer for all of my clients. It's your weekly map to get you out further of the woods.

4. Practice: The Values-led To-do List

Our to-do lists often work poorly for us. They tend to lead us, rather than the other way round. By the time we get to the end of each day, we have hardly any reserves of time or energy left to focus on aligning our lives with our values, so we stay stuck. Here's how to create a to-do list that helps.

1. At the beginning of each week, take a clean sheet of paper and draw a line down the middle to form two columns.
2. At the top of one of these columns write 'Life' and on the other 'Work'.
3. Now draw a horizontal line across the middle of your page.
4. Above this line write 'Important' and below it 'Not Important'.
5. Above the line, in each column, write:
   - those things that are a big yes, or steps on your 'moving the needle' personal or professional projects, which will bring change to your life and bring you into alignment with your values, for instance, the first steps to writing that workshop – remembering to break goals down into smaller tasks;
   - activities that support your physical and mental health – your health is your foundation, without which nothing else is possible;

- anything on a deadline this week, for instance, filing taxes, or someone's birthday.

6. Below the line, write less important activities without an immediate deadline, such as general errands and activities that can wait.

7. If anything doesn't align with your values, or in some way dishonours them, figure out a plan to manage them so you have time for the activities and projects that do, and that support your health. We're all grown-ups, and there are some tasks that we have to do that are important but don't light us up (oh, hello, taxes and invoicing). But as you did with the exercise at the end of Chapter Two, when you ran your activities, habits and invitations through the filter of your bigger yes, you want to give yourself enough time and energy for values-led activities. You can't do that if you are filling your to-do list with other things. It can take time to move to this, so don't beat yourself up if it does. Set your intention and start by setting some boundaries. I have a morning a month for invoicing so it doesn't bleed into the rest of my time. I also make sure I get out into nature at least once a week.

8. At the end of your week, take a look and review. If you notice that you are ticking off mostly items below the line, you are spending too much time on the small stuff. Although completing small, unimportant tasks can feel rewarding in the short term, you are not moving your life

forward or taking care of yourself, and you are avoiding the bigger or trickier stuff. If most of your ticks are on the work side, then work may be encroaching on too much of your life. Commit to finding balance. Be realistic. You may only be able to do one or two things a day. We all have a tendency to overestimate how long it will take us to do something. The important thing is to keep going and build momentum step by step.

If you have been following the exercises and practices so far, then hopefully by now you will have opened up some time and space to get into deeper connection with yourself, found your North Star, built yourself a compass, so you don't get lost, and even the beginnings of a map. But if we keep our eyes glued on our feet as we start taking steps forward to forge a new path, we lose sight of the land on which we stand – the big picture. So in the next chapter, I am going to ask you to have the courage to lift up your gaze and shift perspective. What makes life itself so meaningful is knowing what a gift it is.

5. Shift Perspective and Let Go

If you are living your life right, then there may come a time when you feel frightened. Sometimes because you feel overwhelmed by uncertainty. Sometimes because things happen that you can't control. Truth is, we live our lives within the bounds of a great predicament: we know that one day we will die; we don't want it to happen; and we don't know when it will happen. What greater provocation could there be for the existential anxiety woven into the fabric of our lives? Yet if we have the courage to walk our path *with* that truth *and* our fear, our greatest predicament can be our greatest teacher, guiding us to a deeper sense of purpose as we consider how we want to live in the time we have. You are moving out of the wood with your compass to guide you. Lift up your eyes, see the landscape on which you stand. Your Big I knows that life itself is a gift. Live it the best way you can before you die. In this chapter, you'll explore how appreciating life's preciousness helps you focus on how to do this, accepting the necessary sacrifices you need to make to find your own path with grace, so that at the end of your life you can say, 'I lived a life true to myself.'

Intellectually, we know we are going to die one day. But experiencing the reality of death and fragility of life at close hand can change us at a deeper, more visceral level. Years ago, my dear brother underwent emergency brain surgery, and when hospital visiting hours ended each evening, it ripped out my heart to leave him. I remember walking from the hospital and feeling as if the atoms in the pavement would split apart and I would fall through. It was as if the laws of physics that kept me safe no longer worked. Now I felt the truth in my bones: the people I loved would die, everyone would die, I would die. Up to that moment, I hadn't had to face this, and now that had changed forever. I don't know how, but I took another step forward, and then another, as I headed slowly home.

From that point onwards, I couldn't run from the truth. All I could do was to find the courage to be with it.

Courage in the Face of Our Mortality

We are such extraordinary beings – and we barely appreciate it. If I asked you to write a list of what you appreciate about yourself, and what you appreciate about your loved ones, chances are you'd miss something essential. On a daily basis I miss it myself. Our courage. We live knowing we will die; we love, knowing others will die. It's overwhelming and can fill us with dread. So, understandably, we often manage our fears by avoiding thinking about it at all, and we are encouraged in this by a modern culture that keeps us distracted. Yet without the courage to look up from our Little I lives to the Big I perspective that life is finite and precious, we cut ourselves off from the source of what ultimately gives our life meaning.

Here's a story that illustrates what I mean by courage. I was once on holiday with a friend, who insisted we go whitewater rafting. Personally, the prospect gave me the jitters, but I tagged along anyway – more in fear of humiliation than with unbounded joy. At the raft, our guide asked for volunteers to go in the prow. I held back, so he placed me with another woman in the stern.

Before long, we were crashing through the rapids. The people in the front whooped as the boat crested over one wave before plunging into the seething cauldron below. I felt less thrill, more heart-churning fear. At one point we pulled into a quieter pool by the bank, and it was only then that I heard the sound of sobbing. The woman sitting across from me in the back was having a terrible time. She shook and her face was wet with tears and snot. No one else noticed her over their excited chatter and the noise of the river. I leaned across and rather pointlessly asked her if she was okay. Between heavy sobs, she told me this was her honeymoon, and she had left it to her new husband to plan some fun activities. However, she hadn't let him know that she was terrified of whitewater rafting. You can imagine her horror when he announced a big surprise down by the river. He was so excited, and she so ashamed, that she couldn't bear to admit her fears. Here she was, in her worst nightmare, in the back of an inflatable raft charging down a wild river.

'You must think I am pathetic. I *am* pathetic. Look at everyone else, having a great time, so much more courageous than me.'

'You have to be kidding,' I said. 'You are the bravest person in this boat.'

She did a double-take.

I continued, 'The others aren't afraid, so what does

this mean to them, what have they had to overcome just to be here? You are scared seven ways before breakfast, and you still got in the boat. Lady, I salute you.'

She inhaled, and as she turned towards me, her face glowed.

'Damn, I *am* the bravest person in the boat!'

We set off again and she dug her oar in deep, still scared, but now powered up with the realization of her own courage.

I share this story to help you understand that absence of fear isn't necessarily courage. We fear changing our lives, we fear death and suffering, and we often criticize ourselves for that. We need to credit ourselves for being in the boat, in the midst of a raging river, digging our oars in as we try to steer ourselves to a meaningful life in the knowledge we are ultimately mortal. *This* is courage, because – however you look at it – we are all in the boat.

Building a Better Relationship with Death

It's understandable that the prospect of death frightens us, which is why humans have created practices and mindsets that can help. The philosophical school of Stoicism in third-century BCE Athens had a morning practice which included imagining all the ways you could come to a terrible end that day, which was useful when you faced famine, invasion or the random acts of capricious gods, as well as any number of diseases and their almost equally unpleasant treatments. The classical Greek philosopher Epicurus saw all our anxiety having a root cause in fear of death. In Europe, from medieval to Victorian times, architecture, art and jewellery sometimes featured *memento mori* (which translated from the Latin means 'remember you must die') such as skulls, clocks and hourglasses, to remind people that death walked alongside them, no matter whether they were a peasant, merchant, scholar or king.

Religions also offer ways to contain, relieve or transform our fear. For instance, *maranasati* or contemplation of death is central to Buddhism. In a parable, a young woman, driven to despair by the death of her only child, asked the Buddha if he could bring her back. The Buddha replied, 'Before I can help, you have to gather some white mustard seeds from a family who has never known death, and bring them to me.'

Filled with hope, the woman went from house to house, asking all the families if they had lost anyone. All said yes. Eventually, she returned crestfallen to the Buddha and told him that she couldn't find what he had asked for. As she spoke, she realized that she was not alone, that death is a truth of life for everyone, that life is impermanent. With this realization, she started to become more enlightened.

Our modern technological, consumerist culture doesn't offer us the space or practices to create a healthy relationship with death and our fear of it, with traces only remaining in poetry, religion and psychotherapy, though research shows that mindfully coming to terms with death is essential to living life fully. Without a healthy relationship with our mortality, remembering that this may encompass feeling powerful emotions about it, we might believe that life is, in the face of the reality of death, meaningless. We can feel very frightened and small, which is understandable. But when we can accept our mortality, we receive the gift of a powerful perspective on life, and we can understand that although we cannot choose our circumstances, we can choose our responses to them.

Making Meaning from Knowledge of Death

Alana didn't choose to get cancer. When she was diagnosed in her forties – fit, active and a successful professional – her priorities changed overnight. The foundation of our lives is health, and we often take it for granted until something happens. Alana now had to approach her own health and life in a way that was alien to her. Her diary filled with appointments with oncologists, chemotherapy, nutritionists, blood work and scans. She usually came to me during this period needing a sounding board to help her decide on her plan for treatment, work and life. One day, her demeanour was noticeably different. I could sense she was on the edge of something but was struggling to reach it. With a shaky breath, she asked,

'Can I please talk about death? Everyone is telling me to stay positive, and that's great, but it's as if I am not allowed even to think about death. And . . . the truth is . . . I'm really frightened.'

This was completely understandable. When we can't talk about death, it's as if we don't have permission to feel our own feelings about it. I asked her to tell me what frightened her about death.

'I feel I haven't achieved enough. I thought I would have more time, and now I may not.'

It's hard to walk a mile in someone like Alana's shoes, although we are all on the same path. But, along with her treatment, Alana's encounter with the fragility of life was the initiation that brought her to her own threshold. Imbued with a greater sense of her life's preciousness, she decided to change it. She separated from old scripts about her body's invincibility. She put a stop to the activities which were no longer meaningful, and to striving for status for its own end, and re-entered her own life more richly and deeply. Later, several months after her remission, she told me about the perspective her experience had given her,

'I remember when I was really young sitting in a tree, thinking there is something so clearly good inside, like a diamond, right in the middle of me, and it needs to manifest, and then I will be myself in the world. My life as a young adult was a lot about striving to overcome disadvantages so I could do that.

'When I got sick, it was the first time that I ever really felt mortal, and I had to understand that I couldn't just choose to live however I wanted to, there were constraints. And that actually there are many ways of living a good life.

'I see it now as before and after. It's different mentally, emotionally and spiritually. The striving is very different. It's no longer primarily for me but for others – creating conditions for them to thrive. It surprises me, how much I know now that gives me the ability to respond in situations that I wouldn't have been able to before. I have a sense of purpose, and that definitely makes the diamond a bit shinier.'

She told me that the things which had once brought her joy – travel to exotic places, a busy social life and getting plaudits and pay rises – no longer did so to the same extent. Now she had deeper connection with her family and friends. Her path now is a new one, in which she has discovered meaning not in spite of but because of facing death. Knowing now how precious and short life is, she focuses that diamond on what's important and worries less than she used to. Her mantra is: 'What am I waiting for?'

You don't need to be in the same situation as Alana to ask yourself the same question. If you don't keep in mind that your life will one day end, you can live your life in the false belief that you have all the time in the world. That you don't leaves you with a paradox: life is short, and it is never too late. To help create a meaningful life you need to hold these two things in mind at the same time: you have no control over the finality of your death and more over what you can do with your life. We are not in the waiting room of life. This is it.

Understanding Our Purpose

Alana felt a greater sense of purpose in her life. What do I mean by purpose? Simply put, it is the inner belief that, in whatever way you choose to live your life, you live it authentically, in the best possible way for the unique person you are. You bring your gifts into the world not just in what you do but in who you are, knowing you make an impact or contribution, and wanting to make it a positive one. Why would this matter? People who have a sense of purpose report that they experience greater mastery, meaning and fulfilment in their lives. They also say it helps them deal with life's inevitable challenges. The philosopher Friedrich Nietzsche wrote that 'he who has a *why* to live for can bear almost any *how*'. I like thinking of purpose as our 'why' – it demystifies it, and makes it more relatable and applicable in our everyday lives. Having a why gives you a deep well of energy to draw upon when things go well – and when they don't. Purpose is a part of your compass. When you are in the middle of a storm or feeling lost, reminding yourself of your why helps you orient yourself again. You can say to yourself, 'This is what I am here for. This is why I do what I do. This is the difference I can make in my own and others' lives.'

You don't always decide your purpose; you can discover it. Sometimes a need arises in the world and what you already know and are crystallizes to meet it. During the pandemic lockdown when Mia – the dancer and teacher who shared her story for this book – lost her work, her home and her sense of identity tied to them, she decided to spend time with her brother and his wife, who was in the final stages of a terminal illness. It was a revelation.

'We're often so busy and self-important, we don't really know the people close to us. How did I not know my brother was suffering so badly? I thought of all my years practising meditation and cultivating a spiritual life, and realized I could bring that to the situation. I ended up helping to care for my brother and sister-in-law, organizing the funeral and being the celebrant. I didn't ask to do it. They were just situations I was put into and I said, "Oh, okay, all right." '

What she used were gifts and abilities that she had cultivated for other reasons. But when the moment came, another purpose became clear. She was called. She decided to retrain as an interfaith minister so that she could serve more people. Life will sometimes offer you moments when you too are called to a bigger purpose. Even if it doesn't, you can still shift perspective to start to connect with the bigger picture of the purpose of your life.

If you're reading this and worrying that you are yet to work out what your purpose is, don't worry. When I coach someone, the most useless question I can ask is, 'What is your purpose?' It's too overwhelming, and it is tempting to tackle it as you would an intellectual puzzle, when, in fact, brainpower won't get you very far. But if we shift our perspective to the end of our lives, the question comes more clearly into focus, as you'll discover in this next exercise. So don't fret at the seeming enormity of the concept. Carry it more lightly. It might be simpler than you imagine.

As you're contemplating the end of your life, go gently. I invite clients to imagine a scale between one and ten, with one being not anxious at all and ten being very upset or even traumatized. Some days it's too much, especially if you have recently lost someone yourself, for instance. Don't go above six, please. You might feel some emotions even then. There's nothing wrong, don't worry – you may have touched on something you care about. The Little I keeps you busy and distracted to avoid these deeper parts of yourselves. Gently breathe and welcome those emotions in, by softly saying 'hello'. That shy deer of your Big I is here.

Exercise: At the End

1. Close your eyes and take a few gentle breaths.
2. Visualize yourself towards the end of your life, as an old person. You are in a place where you feel comfortable and calm, perhaps in a garden or a favourite armchair. Let gratitude fill you.
3. Ask yourself:
   - What are your most precious memories?
   - What did people learn from you?
   - How do you want to be remembered?
   - How did you make the world a better place, in what you did and who you were? What legacy are you leaving behind?
4. Imagine that you have something near you to remind you of the impact you made. It could be a picture, an ornament, a piece of furniture or clothing. What is it there to remind you of? Try not to overthink this. Note down what comes up as it will give you some pointers towards your purpose. It may take some time, so don't judge yourself if it

doesn't spring forth at once. Maybe you have such an item or could find or create it. If you do, then keep it somewhere you can see it in your everyday life.

5. Take a few gentle breaths, breathing in gratitude and out gratitude. When you are ready, open your eyes. Write down what you experienced in your journal.

In doing this exercise, you might notice – along with many of my clients – that what comes up tends not to be lofty, and hardly ever a job title. A job is a *vehicle* for your purpose. We are conditioned to think we'll find our purpose through work, but it's much bigger than that, and you can live it through any or all aspects of your life. When I first viewed my life from the perspective of its end, I had a clear sense of connecting people – and myself – with our hearts. I bring this into action every day as a coach. I could do this if I was an architect, sales manager, teacher, shop assistant or in other jobs. I do this as a friend, partner, sister and daughter. I can do this on the bus or on the street. I do this with myself. My purpose brings the essence of who I am together with what I have learned and how I have grown in my life, not in spite of my struggles but because of them. If purpose is about *why* we do what we do, values are *how* we choose to live our purpose. I live my purpose whether I coach someone or find myself in the back of a raft with them. When you walk your own path, there's no division or separation. Who you are and how you decide to be in the world are one and the same.

Many of us can minimize the impact we have on others and in the world, which again reduces the meaning we feel our lives have. 'What difference do I make?' we ask ourselves. It's as if we imagine we are separate from the world and people in it, when we are all connected. I want you to realize that whoever you are, you do have an impact, even though you might not see the results. Sometimes life offers you the gift of being made aware of the difference you made. And even if it doesn't, it doesn't mean you didn't.

Your purpose is suffused into what might be – on the surface – ordinary, rather than grand achievements that gain the validation of masses. I celebrate the ordinary. I want avenues named after people who go up and down supermarket aisles, filling orders for people unable to do it themselves. I want hymns sung to those who take care of an elderly parent or who sit with a grieving friend. Let's start a petition to have plaques put up in the places where someone took a few minutes to mentor a young colleague or help a child with homework, or looked up from their phone to notice someone who was struggling and gave them a hand and a kind word. Most of all, I want us not to think we need to seek lives less ordinary when we cross the threshold to find our own paths, as if the alternative lacks purpose. We have an impact, just in being here at all, even if we don't see evidence of it. Even after we have departed, we leave something behind. How we chose to live our lives – the actions we took, the examples we set – will filter down. We are all leaders. This, finally, is the purpose we all have: to live, knowing we will die, but in some way having an impact on a future we won't live to witness.

The Uses of Regret

If we linger a while longer at the end of our lives, we will find another important question to ask ourselves: what will we regret not doing or being? Regret has a bad reputation, but, used well, it can be a great tool that can help us find our own path.

Exercise: Anticipation of Regret

1. Close your eyes, take a few gentle breaths and imagine yourself again as an elderly person in a place, as before, where you feel calm and at ease.
2. When you look back on your life from this perspective, what do you regret not doing and being?
3. When you are ready, take a few breaths and open your eyes.
4. Take a pen and journal about what came up.
5. Now ask yourself what you can you do now and in the next year so that you won't create these regrets? Write this down and make a commitment to act on it.

As I get older, I realize that it is probably impossible to live a life without some regrets. There will be roads not taken, and lapses of kindness, clarity, wisdom or courage, for instance. We are human and imperfect, we have to make choices from where we are at the time, not what we realized later; we can't do everything and we sometimes screw up the things we do do. Remember, life isn't a project to perfect. But because fear of loss is a strong motivator in our lives, when we visualize potential future regrets if we do not live our authentic lives, then this can lead us to positive action. We can focus on what's important, and maybe drop the small stuff. *Because* our time is finite, there is no time like the present to start living our lives to minimize the regrets we will live into otherwise. As Charley, the former military officer, told me,

'When I'm ninety and in a nursing home, I want to be that woman that says, do you remember the time that I did whatever?'

At the end of your life, you won't be glad you spent all that time scrolling social media or worrying. At the end of our lives, we all will want to have lived a life true to ourselves. It's never too late. What that means is that we have to learn to let go of what doesn't ultimately matter in our lives.

Letting Go

As the bereaved mother in the Buddhist parable discovered, death is a reality for everyone. Within our lives, there are also little deaths – endings, sacrifices and choices we need to make to let go of what no longer serves us, so we can find our own path.

Yasmin moved from one career as an activist to another as a successful writer, and she had to let go of what was enabling her to avoid her initiation call, and loosen her attachment to aspects of her identity.

'Part of my journey transitioning from one career to another was to identify what I was using to numb out the discomfort, and trying to stop that in order to create the space to listen to what needs to come out, what helps. I personally found it quite terrifying. I was so attached to my identity and who I was and what that represented within my circle of friends or in my community.'

When we try to hold on to our old lives, and when we can't accept the need for these little deaths, finding our own path is harder. Sacrifice is hard. When we start moving out of the woods, we often have to give up aspects of our lives – beliefs, habits, validation, old identities, associations and attachments that we are used to, and without which we wonder who we are and how we might cope. These may have kept us held in place, feeling safe and approved of, no matter how uncomfortable or unfulfilled. But there comes a time, at the threshold, when we need to make a choice, as Maria reflected, after leaving her marriage,

'I think it's very hard when you've done something for years to give up on it. But in every battle there comes a point where you go, "Is it worth the casualties any more? Is it worth the losses?"'

Is the juice worth the squeeze? Sometimes it isn't a choice. Mia's son left for university, and, during the pandemic, she had to move from the home she had known and later caught an infection in her foot, which meant she might not be able to return to her work in dance. Her life was going to be very different from now on.

'Everything that I had known kind of completely fell away. All my identities. I think I went through a real sort of death process of all the things I had put a lot of energy into to create.'

What do you need to let go of, so you can find your own path? In Chapter One, you started to notice the scripts and 'shoulds' that run your life. In Chapter Two, you noticed the habits, shortcuts, busyness, short-term rewards and a few more of those inner 'shoulds' and loyalties we have to out-of-date selves. If you have identified a few you'd like to let go, write them down in the exercise below, as well as anything else that comes up.

Exercise: Letting Go

1. Write down a few things you'd like to let go.
   Here are some ideas:
   - Habits (doing, being, thinking).
   - Things you can't change.
   - Ways of dealing with things that aren't working.
   - Your desire to keep things the same, even though they are changing.
2. Read your list and ask yourself, what is the one thing you could let go of today that would make the most immediate change to your life? Start small: it could be an overpacked diary; if so, your next step is to go through it and cancel appointments. It might be a habit of

rumination. Can you notice when you're in it
and start practising saying 'stop' to yourself.

There isn't a magic wand you can wave that will instantly
evaporate anything you want to let go of. Writing a list of
things we want to let go of is a start, but actually letting go
is harder. Every day I notice things I am clinging to and
recommit. It's human to want to hold on. What I ask you
to do in writing down what you'd like to let go of is to
become aware, be kind to yourself, rather than beating
yourself up, and choose to keep noticing them when they
come up, so that you can let them go again.

When we remember that life is itself impermanent, we
can bring a little more ease into letting go, a little less
resistance to the natural flow in which things come and
go. What can also help is a simple practice that helps us
notice this flow, and feel safe and supported.

'Hello, Goodbye' Practice for Letting Go

1. Find a place to sit on a chair with your feet on
   the floor, or on the floor on a cushion or rolled
   towel with legs crossed. Let your eyes close.
   Centre: belly, jaw, expand.
2. Imagine that the earth is gently pushing up to
   support your body. You don't need to do
   anything – you might see if you can relax your
   body by 10 per cent, knowing it is supported by
   the earth. If this feels hard, and if you struggle
   to feel safe, which can be especially difficult if

you have experienced trauma, then take time to feel your body supported before you move on to the next steps. Notice how the chair or floor supports you. Feel the way your feet contact the ground. There's no rush.

3. Move your awareness slowly up through your body from where it connects with the ground: feet, legs, pelvis, abdomen, torso, spine, arms, hands, neck and head. Feel that every part of your body is supported from the ground up.

4. Breathe gently in, and, as you do, say silently to yourself, 'Hello.'

5. Exhale and, as you softly let the breath go, think, 'Goodbye.' Repeat this for the next few breaths.

6. Once you have done this a few times, notice any sensation in your body – a tingle, heat, cold, itching, tension or relaxation. Focus on one. If you can't feel anything, just pay attention to your breath. As you breathe in, say to yourself, 'Hello,' and as you exhale, let go of your focus on that sensation and say, 'Goodbye.' Repeat with the other sensations, one at a time, as many or few as you wish.

7. Next, bring your attention to your thoughts, and as one pops up, say, 'Hello,' as you breathe in and, 'Goodbye,' as you exhale and drop your focus on it. Do the same for any impulses you notice, for instance, to get up and do something else.

8. Take your awareness outside of your body. Do you notice any sounds? Place your attention on one and repeat the cycle above.

9. Finally, drop your focus on anything and sit for a few minutes. Allow any sensations, thoughts or sounds as they arise. Open to them without getting hooked and following any of them down the rabbit hole into stories of what should or shouldn't be happening.

When you are ready, end the practice and check in on how you feel. Get into the habit of doing this whenever you feel you need to let go of something or when you notice you're holding on to something.

On a daily basis, we suffer because we fear loss. What we actually lose is the big picture. We cling to and worry about things that are less important, which brings more suffering, and we lose inner calm and acceptance. If we can accept our fears without letting them overwhelm us, we can focus on what's important with a sense of purpose. This truth changes our perspective and helps us appreciate life itself. Every day is a gift.

6. Replenish Your Wells

What you choose to do with the gift of life depends a great deal on the energy you have to live it. We sometimes forget we are part of nature and our energy ebbs and flows in our own seasons. After a period of energetic activity, we harvest the fruits, recover and plant the seeds for spring. Sometimes, following an interval of patience after planting those seeds, we are called upon to open out again to the world, our new shoots reaching out for light and nourishment in our personal spring. One of the ways I go easier on myself is by remembering that it would be unnatural to expect that I can live an eternal summer in all aspects of my life all the time. I suspect the root of this expectation lies in unhelpful analogies about our energy. We talk of 'switching off', as if we are machines. Rather than our energy being sourced through a constant mains supply, imagine you have several wells that need replenishment. When one is low, you can draw from another, but this too depletes, unless you top it up. You need to pay attention to your energy, because you are deciding what you are going to give it to and what not, and feeling more energized is one of the ways you know you're on your path. When you are exhausted, you'll be more stressed, more likely to default to your old one and get caught up again in the Little I life of automatic behaviour. You risk losing both your compass and sight of the big picture.

You're now deep in the process of finding your own path. One of the struggles you'll encounter is that your old life will tug on your sleeve, demand attention and drain the energy you need to create a secure foothold. Nothing but nothing will change in your life unless and until you set boundaries around this insistent clamour and have the energy to tend your new shoots. In this chapter, you'll discover how to protect and replenish your wells of energy by developing understanding and discernment around what drains and diminishes and what energizes and enlarges you, so you can choose where to focus your precious inner resources with each step out of the woods.

Why Are We So Tired?

If you feel tired and drained, you're not alone. Many of those who find themselves at the threshold – wanting to make a choice to take a different, more authentic path – are there because their current lives now exhaust rather than energize them. If the craziness of our lives isn't tiring enough, as we naturally age, we might not be able to stay up late, eat and drink what we once enjoyed, or keep company with the same people, and still be bright-eyed and bushy-tailed the next day. I knew my menopause had arrived when, no matter where I was or what I was doing, I could have lain down right there and then and taken a three-hour nap. I would make excuses why I couldn't meet people in the evening, but rarely revealed it was because I wanted to be in bed by nine thirty.

There is a cultural shame about ageing and our need for rest, and we internalize this. Yet ageing is part of the natural journey of our lives, and rest is essential to have energy to do the important things in life. Our needs change.

Another reason you might be dragging yourself out of bed is that, although you might have once been energized by work achievements, for instance, values shift as you grow and age, and quality of life, purpose, balance and meaningful connections matter more. Evidence also points towards these being sources of greater meaning and well-being in our lives as we grow older. You built the life you are living for a previous version of yourself, and as you grow, that life will become out of date and so feel less energizing. If you're still living your life aligned to an old North Star, you're going to feel weary.

We are often not aware of how much energy we expend, whilst not paying attention to our need to replenish. Burnout can bring us to the threshold with a crash. Ali is a woman, just turned sixty, who has had multiple chapters in her life – from teacher, designer, facilitator to now nurturing her own creativity. To make this vital change in her life she needed to notice where her own energy was going:

'I was gifting my energy resource to the needs of others and neglecting my own. And my well-being really suffered for that. I burned out. It was kind of inevitable.'

For Adam, the games developer, the first step to finding his own path required a period of recovery:

'I am super burned out and not very good at being kind to myself. I have been operating in a mode of endurance for so long that I've forgotten there's any other way of living.'

I hear this so often, it seems to have become normal. Even if you don't hit burnout (and most of us aren't even aware of the signs, so I have added a list at the end of this book – see Appendix 2), here are a couple of questions to reflect upon, which reveal your patterns of energy.

Journal Questions

- What words would you use to describe how you feel about the weekend?
- As you approach a holiday, what do you look forward to?

Depending on your responses, you may notice you have a pattern of stress and recovery, week-by-week living for the weekend crash or the next holiday – and you are not alone. Our current lifestyles ask a great deal from us, and often seem to give back less and less in return. Although you may want to change this, the irony is you are probably too exhausted by your current habits and patterns to do anything about it. But you can.

Put Your Own Oxygen Mask On First

When you get on a plane, the safety briefing will tell you – in the unlikely case of an emergency – to put your own oxygen mask on before assisting anyone else. You need to be told this because your instinct is often to do the opposite. To find your own path, you need to put your own mask on first – refilling your reserves, setting boundaries and managing your energy so you can move from *stress and recovery* to *awareness and replenishment*.

The good news is that there are practices that will help, but unless you know what affects your personal energy patterns and needs, and create your own plan, it's like trying to jive when a slow dance plays.

When my clients map their personal energy levels and commit to their own replenishment activities, they feel ownership, lightness and playfulness. It's a dance in which you become skilled in noticing what's needed, rather than a piece of sheet music you slavishly follow. Life isn't about getting everything done, it isn't an endless list of tasks, although it certainly can feel that way sometimes. It's about living more fully as a human. I hope you're excited at the prospect. Let's start by revealing more about you than you may realize.

The Eight Types of Energy

Nowadays you can buy energy bars, drinks and supplements. We talk about not having the energy to do something. Although we use a catch-all term, I use the idea of having eight different kinds of energy with clients, because then they can discern which are drained and need replenishing, like wells from which we draw throughout our day and need to refill. Finding your own path requires all of them. As always, I am not suggesting there is a way you *should* be – no endless high-energy summer. Sometimes we need to accept where we are with grace and compassion, so that we can work with rather than against reality, and can replenish in more nourishing ways. For instance, I need to accept my occasional brain fog and off-days, and a lovely client of mine who is recovering from long Covid has had to accept her need for convalescence, instead of trying to do the same things she could before she contracted the virus.

Here are eight different wells of energy, with some questions to help identify each and the differences between them more clearly in yourself. If you discover more wells, or want to combine some, or if different names make sense to you, then great, amend your list to make it work for you. If you are suffering unexplained chronic or sudden changes in energy in any area, please check with a medical professional, as there may be an underlying condition which needs addressing.

Take up your journal and reflect on the questions I include.

Physical Energy

This is your foundation, affected by nutrition, exercise and sleep. Age, illness and chronic conditions or impairments will also affect your physical energy, as will menstrual cycles and the menopause, so please don't measure yourself against a one-size fits all template. This is just the first step to noticing how you are and what will help.

Journal Questions

- How physically strong do you feel?
- What's your stamina and stability like? How long can you walk before you feel tired, and do you feel steady on your feet?
- What about your flexibility? You don't need to touch your toes, but can you reach for things you need?
- How often do you get out of breath or raise your heart rate, and how long does it take you to recover?
- Do you usually wake up feeling re-energized? You don't need to have eight hours sleep every night. Does your sleep pattern work for you?
- How often do you get ill or feel physically run down?

Cognitive Energy

How mentally sharp and focused do you feel? Again, let's let go of the idea that we need to remember everything all the time. I struggle to remember friends' names nowadays, but I don't stress about it. However, when I am trying to remember too many things or am too distracted, forgetting my keys and being locked out would be a bigger problem.

Journal Questions

- Can you remember where you left things?
- Can you recall names of people and places?
- Are you able to hold two things in your mind at the same time?
- Are you able to focus on one thing for a period of time? When we multi-task, this gets very stretched. Are you able to pay attention and to switch it consciously?

Intellectual Energy

I am not talking about understanding the laws of thermodynamics (although good for you, if you can), more your ability to read an article or listen to someone, comprehend what they are saying – especially if it requires seeing things from another standpoint – and apply novel, critical thinking, without resorting to easy equivalences or knee-jerk responses. In other words, are you able to *think*?

Journal Questions

- Can you comprehend ideas and points of view that are new, complex or not your own?
- Can you respond thoughtfully, and be okay with ambiguity, uncertainty and not-knowing?

Creative Energy

This is about imagination and innovation, and it has nothing to do with being a 'creative person', having a creative job or having stunningly original ideas. We are all creative. When faced with something that needs a new approach, we create solutions.

Journal Questions

- Are you able to take two or more ideas, thoughts or things and combine them to create something new?
- When there's a new situation or problem, are you able to address it creatively?

Spiritual Energy

Some draw this from their religious faith, beliefs, philosophies and practices. But even if you are not religious, you have the capacity for spiritual energy.

Journal Questions

- Do you feel energized by a sense of purpose?
- Do you feel connected to something bigger than yourself?
- Are you able to draw energy from connection to a higher power or perspective?

Social Energy

Extroverts feel energized around people; introverts can feel drained more easily but often still need and long for social connection. Most of us move along a sliding scale somewhere in between, rather than being fixed. We can feel energized around people who share our values, for instance, but not with people who don't. We can feel energized with people for a couple of hours, but then need to duck out and have time alone.

Journal Questions

- Do you feel energized around other people? How many? Which kinds of people?
- At a certain point, do you start to feel drained around others?
- Do you need time alone afterwards to recover?

Sexual Energy

This is not about having sex for hours or experiencing multiple orgasms. It's the life force which pulls us to another, and that heat and aliveness by which we are in touch with our sexual self, whether or not we are having sex or are in partnerships. It can be affected naturally by hormone cycles. If low, it can be a sign that our wells may be empty in other areas. Self-criticism, the absence of self-love and care are also signs this can be running low. Along with all the other energy forms, this may naturally change as you age, so don't beat yourself with a model of what it should feel and look like. Many people I have worked with notice that this energy can shift into greater creative energy.

Journal Questions

- Do you feel aroused by a sexual partner?
- Do you feel excited at the prospect of sex?
- Do you sense your own sexual energy, and feel vital aliveness, whether you have a partner or not?
- Do you experience boundaried sexual energy? For instance, is it difficult to pay attention to what else might be happening if you are turned on? Are you able to slow down and read and respond to another's needs when you are?

Emotional Energy

If you feel drained after a difficult conversation with someone, this is the well you have been drawing from. It can be affected by how we feel about our lives, work, relationships and ourselves. It can also be drained when we don't have boundaries and give too much to others, as well as by the algorithm of social media that thrives on your outrage, entices you to jump into arguments and offers lots of ways for you to feel bad about yourself and others.

Journal Questions

- Can you listen attentively while someone talks to you about their feelings?
- Can you pay attention to your own feelings, or do you tend to avoid them?
- Can you feel healthy anger, without being overwhelmed and still be able to communicate assertively and let it go? Can you feel joy, without relying on drugs or alcohol or external stimulation from people or events around you? Or do you feel flat, no matter what?
- Can you notice when you're giving too much, and ease back and prioritize your needs?

As you read through the list of different kinds of energy, remember, you are not aiming for a goal. This is about noticing and discerning.

Practice: Your Energy Diary

Keep a daily energy diary for a month. Each night, note down what energized and drained you, and write down which type of energy you feel was affected and why. Here are the headings to keep it simple:

- Fills me
- Drains me
- I am at my best when . . .

You'll start to notice that the level in each well affects many others. When you are physically exhausted, you'll feel depleted socially and sexually, for instance. When your spiritual energy is low, you may struggle to be creatively inspired, which is why meditation or taking an intentional mindful walk in nature can help. Many find having a small ritual to connect them to a higher power, perhaps symbolized by lighting incense or a candle on a home altar opens up the creative well. For Devon, his Buddhist beliefs and practices energize him like a river bringing nourishment to his whole life:

'Spirituality is the creative force of my life that is positive, dynamic, really self-serving in the truest possible, authentic way. I feel everybody has it. We might call it different things, but I think we all have this potential within us to draw out of our lives something which we didn't think was there and then use that to drive us through life.'

As his experience shows, high levels in one well will nourish your energy in others. When your intellectual energy gauge is high, you will be gathering the input to be creative, and when you feel cognitively sharp, you'll be more able to give attentive emotional energy to someone or something. Replenish one and that will affect others. There's a wealth of evidence that running, swimming and cycling can clear the mind, yoga and Pilates help concentration and relaxation, walking boosts your mood, and all these activities help reduce stress and anxiety. Think of these wells as all being connected through the deeper water table.

What affects your own personal wells of energy? Here's what I have noticed from keeping an energy diary.

Again, this is what works for me. The important thing is to be honest about what works and doesn't for you *now* based on your diary, not on an out-of-date belief.

- *Physical*
  - *Fills me*: yoga, nature, walking, dancing, eating healthily, mainly fresh food, drinking water, regular routines of sleep and rest, swimming in the sea, getting outside in the daylight.
  - *Drains me*: travel, sitting for hours at a time, extended screen use (especially late at night), eating heavily in the evening, alcohol and processed foods, late nights, grey winter days.
  - *I am at my best*: when I don't overdo it or try to do too much, when I include some yoga and walking several times a week, and longer walks at least every other weekend, when I eat a balanced diet and have my main meal early, when I didn't drink alcohol the night before, and when I get off screens by 9 p.m.
- *Cognitive*
  - *Fills me*: all of the above, plus meditation and mindfulness, coming off automatic.
  - *Drains me*: again, all of the above, plus multi-tasking, too much information incoming at once, too many hours a day with clients, facilitating classes online in the evening.
  - *I am at my best*: in the morning, when I slow down and have a set time for tasks and errands, after rest, sleep, exercise or going outside for fresh air.

- *Intellectual*
  - *Fills me*: stimulation such as reading a good book, listening to an interesting podcast or having a chat about things that matter with a friend who is knowledgeable and will challenge me, learning.
  - *Drains me*: trying to focus for too long, engaging in divisive debates, reading lots of upsetting news online.
  - *I am at my best*: in the afternoon, when I have done all of my tasks and have uninterrupted time to focus.
- *Creative*
  - *Fills me*: reading, walks in nature, inspiring conversations, seeing the beauty in small things, taking photos, light housework and tending plants, which is when ideas pop up.
  - *Drains me*: doing the same thing day in, day out, lack of stimulation.
  - *I am at my best*: once I have all my smaller admin, health and connection tasks out of the way, and I switch distractions and notifications off, so I can focus for a few hours.
- *Spiritual*
  - *Fills me*: time alone in nature, spiritual practice such as meditation, spiritual reading, contemplation of the sacredness of life, and practising gratitude, singing, listening to uplifting music, sharing with like-minded people.

- *Drains me*: negative thinking, days of tick-box tasks, blaming others.
- *I am at my best*: when I take time to do some practice in the morning, evening and weekends.

- *Social*
  - *Fills me*: Connecting with good friends.
  - *Drains me*: Networking, too much noise and activity around me, not being understood, too much exposure to people.
  - *I am at my best*: during the day or until mid-evening, I connect meaningfully one-on-one or with small groups of good friends, when I know I can leave when I need to.

- *Sexual*
  - *Fills me*: touch, laughter, dance, playfulness, noticing and appreciating other beautiful, vibrant, authentic people.
  - *Drains me*: isolation, shame, self-judgement, comparing myself unfavourably to other people.
  - *I am at my best*: when I appreciate myself, when I open myself to the appreciation of others, when I get out in the sun, when I wear clothes that I feel good in.

- *Emotional*
  - *Fills me*: when someone listens to me without interrupting or trying to fix me, when I do work I genuinely believe makes a difference to another person and/or the world.

- *Drains me*: when I am hard on myself, when I take things too personally, when I take too much responsibility for others, when I have a difficult conversation with someone, when something isn't easily resolvable, when I try to do or be anything that I don't feel aligned with, when I follow a script not my own.
- *I am at my best*: when I accept myself and practise self-compassion.

When you have a greater sense of your personal wells of energy, care for them. When I ask you to notice what drains you, I don't mean that you should always avoid it. You can't avoid wells running low at times, just as you can't avoid grey days – especially if you live in northern Europe, as I do. You also don't want to avoid a difficult conversation or uncomfortable feelings. Furthermore, bosses, kids and family have a tendency to make demands on your energy, and it's not always possible or advisable to ask them to come back later. But we need to appreciate the effect this has on us, and to replenish ourselves afterwards.

Taking Action

I hope you've found this energy audit insightful, and perhaps revealing. This isn't just about knowing more about yourself, though. You've done some greater inner work here to build your awareness; now you're going to put this into action in your life so you have the energy to find and walk your own path. Remember, when you're tired and drained, you are more likely to default back to old, familiar ways of doing and being – even if they don't serve you.

Practice: Manage Your Energy

- Plan your time to suit your energy patterns as much as possible. If you are most creative in the morning, at the start of the week or at a certain time of the month, for instance, then schedule time for this then. If you are too tired to listen to a friend or partner after a day's work, schedule time at the weekend when you have replenished your emotional energy.
- Commit to replenishing, set boundaries so you don't drop this, and keep these activities above the line in your weekly Values-led To-do list from Chapter Four. You cannot keep draining your wells and expect to have energy in other areas of your life.
- If possible, give things that drain you a limited, scheduled time when they will have minimum impact on other things on which you want to focus. After much trial and error, I tend not to go to social events during the week – with some exceptions, of course, so that I can be more present for my clients and for writing.

It's not a rigid internal command-and-control structure but a dance in which you notice what affects you.

Small steps matter. Remember how in Chapter Two you switched off autopilot to make better tiny choices and give yourself the time and space you need to connect with your deeper self? Similarly, I want you to see how managing your energy with small choices will help you find your path. Is there one small change you could make this week to replenish a well of energy that needs your care?

Even taking small breaks helps. The joy of small steps is that they have a tendency to lead to others, as Maria discovered.

A warm, kind American, she left a job that made her unhappy, moved to the country and ended her marriage. Any one of those would be a big change. But at the beginning of her journey, she couldn't see a path to changing her life, although knew she wanted to. At the threshold, she realized she had to take small first steps to bring more clarity into her life, so she could work out her bigger steps. To do that, she changed a habit that was draining her physical, cognitive and emotional energy wells.

'When I made the decision to stop drinking, I knew that if I just kept doing it until I fell asleep every night, I was going to fall into a stupor, get depressed and nothing would change.'

Within a few weeks of quitting, clarity paid her a visit and set up home in her life. With more wells replenished, she could not only see the changes she needed to make but also had the energy to do something about it. And a well she had been neglecting filled up with spiritual energy.

'I walk every day in the woods, look at the trees, stop and think about the interconnectedness of all of that's happening in nature. I feed myself. It's corny to say it, but I think of Louis Armstrong's "What a Wonderful World" because it's so true.'

Your New Mantra

I don't have the energy I used to – physically and some-times cognitively too. But ageing has also given me new superpowers. Now I only focus on those things I feel truly aligned with. I let go of the small stuff that drained me. I don't see time resting or walking as time off but have reframed it as time replenishing myself.

I have a new mantra you can borrow, even if you are not a woman in her fifties: 'Fuck that.' The late nights that lead to me feeling blurry, unfocused and physically rough the following day? Fuck that. At the end of my life, I don't want to regret too many days spent with avoidable exhaustion. My life is precious, and yours is too. The time I spent posting online to have the dopamine-adrenaline hit of getting likes? Unless I want to say something in line with my core values, fuck that. Bending myself like a pretzel to keep others happy? Holding myself back for fear of being too big for others to bear? Wearing high heels? You guessed it.

Now, I suspect that at any point up to now, and maybe especially with this new mantra, there may be a bit of resistance from within. Change has a way of provoking the choir of inner critics and saboteurs that arise whenever you step out of your comfort zone, so hold tight if this feels hard for you. I get it, 100 per cent. Help is at hand in the next chapter. Of course, I also recommend you cultivate a 'Fuck, yes' attitude. Being clear about my needs and boundaries, and communicating them to people? Telling those I care about that I love them? Oh yes. For every choice, ask does this diminish or enlarge me, is there a Big Yes? Choose where to invest your precious inner resources and you'll clear your way to finding your own path.

7. Make Peace with Inner Critics and Saboteurs

If finding your own path was simple, then you'd probably be doing it already and I'd stop writing and set you loose upon your future. However strong and clear your intentions, however aligned you are with your values and purpose, however masterfully you manage your energy, you'll still face obstacles, and some of the most challenging arise from within. When you step out of your comfort zone to create change in your life, there's a part of you that prefers the comfort of familiarity, wants to keep you safely in it, and will resist. One of the ways it does this is through the chorus of inner critics and saboteurs that activates, clusters around the new life that wants to emerge and can reduce all your confidence, visions and intentions to ashes. You cannot find your own path without having some ways to tackle them, so that they don't vandalize your attempts to create a more meaningful life.

I ask my clients to pay attention to two types of inner voices that tend to show up. Inner critics are the ones that harshly judge you. Saboteurs are part of the same family; however, rather than being critical, they whisper in your ear sometimes quite seductively, undermining your best intentions by disempowering you, so you avoid taking responsibility for your life and writing your story another way. They have the same effect as the critics: you stay in your comfort zones, live your Little I life according to your old scripts, and you suffer anxiety. I'll give you a fuller introduction to the family later – and ways to manage them.

Though I wouldn't blame you for wanting to banish them, I am not going to suggest this for two reasons. First, in my own life I have never found a way to do that completely, and I can't pretend I can help you to do something I haven't been able to do myself. Second, they are part of you, and rejecting them means rejecting a part of yourself, and a little compassion, curiosity and even humour will help you deal with them better than self-hatred. I know they sound unforgiving, judgemental or undermining, but these inner voices developed in your past to protect you, and might actually be useful if you form a better relationship with them and dial down their harshness and avoidance tactics. And when you stay in control, rather than giving them power, you strengthen your wiser, more mature, compassionate, creative and capable Big I self. Remember what I said in Chapter Five about real courage being getting in the boat, even though you're afraid? Your inner critics and saboteurs don't wave you off from the bank. They are in the boat with you. But you don't have to give them the tiller and oars. Those stay in your hands. This chapter is going to help you keep hold of them.

As with all the practices in this book, the ones in this chapter won't just help you find your own path, they are also fundamental to walking it. When you can accept all of yourself – including the more troublesome parts – your life will be more meaningful because it won't be reliant on a limited, shiny version of yourself but on a more whole, imperfect but acceptable you – and when you can accept your own humanity, you can better accept that of others.

Trust me when I tell you that you are not alone. Writing this book has been less a triumph of my knowledge and creativity and more a daily conversation with my critics and saboteurs to get them out of the chair – as I'll share in the next chapter. It helps me to know that making anything worthwhile happen in my life isn't down to their absence but because I know better how to deal with them. Keep that in mind as you read on.

Noticing Their Power

It's rare for me to have a day without a visit from my own inner critics and saboteurs. Whenever I feel vulnerable, they pipe up. Here's an example of a classic attack. I used to experience painful periods. What was even worse than the pain, however, was the suffering my inner critic caused. It barraged me:

'Look at you, whimpering. You're pathetic. It's just period pain; it's not as if it serious. You're just weak.'

I felt every word like a knife in my heart. How typical of an inner critic to weaponize a vulnerability and shame me for it. I didn't even notice it was an inner critic speaking, I just believed it was the truth, which is how they seize so much power from us. To avoid the shame, I would try to tough it out – not just with my periods; in life too I rarely asked for help, believing that was weakness. It wasn't until I was camping solo one night, enduring the pain and martyring myself for hours, that I began to notice how I was speaking to myself. As well as the critic beating me up, there was another, more subtle voice in there too – my sneaky saboteur: 'It's crazy to camp alone; it's impossible. How could you expect to do it? Who said it was a good idea? They don't have to deal with what you do. They don't understand, nobody does. You should just quit now. You can always tell people you did it, to save face. If you tell them you hung on in there with all this pain, you'll sound like a badass.' The lack of distractions in a field in the middle of the night isolated the inner voices that ruled my actions, mood, confidence, connections and well-being.

With the dawn, another, kinder and more grown-up voice broke through the noise.

'Hey, you know what? You're in pain and vulnerable. I love you. Please go and get some food and painkillers. After that you can choose if you want to continue.'

What I realized then has never left me, and I don't believe it ever will. I didn't have to give the critic or the saboteur power. A wiser and more compassionate part of me also wanted to speak, and I could choose to listen. This is the voice you'll start to build a stronger relationship with in this chapter and the next. It's in you, as it is in me.

A Short History of Inner Critics and Saboteurs

Everyone I coach has inner critics and saboteurs, which is hardly surprising when you consider they are trying something new and challenging in finding their own path, which understandably stirs up vulnerability. I have found it helps to know about some of the theories of the history and original purpose of these inner voices, partly so you don't see yourself as weird, weak and deficient for having them, and to help you separate from the misguided belief that they represent reality.

When you were very small, you were defenceless. It's often different in the non-human world. Within minutes of birth, a foal or calf is on its feet and able to stand and walk, albeit unsteadily. This ability helps them survive; they need to be able to stay close to their mother and the herd for food and protection. Newborn human babies, on the other hand, are not renowned for standing and walking unaided, let alone keeping up with the human herd. So what helped you survive? Developmental psychologists have discovered that a baby can recognize their primary caregiver within a few minutes of entry into the world. It's an essential survival mechanism. Because you were so vulnerable when young, you needed to bond with the person who was going to protect you, feed you and keep you warm and safe. That person or people had to do that, with some sacrifice, for years. In short, you survived because you were loved.

Some of you will have had difficult relationships with your parents or caregivers and may not have felt very cared for and protected. I know how painful this is, and that it can be the source of great struggles throughout life if the people you looked to for safety were the ones who most imperilled you, even if this was because of their own struggles. As a child, you had very little choice in the matter. The best thing I can do – apart from send you a virtual hug – is help you discover and practise what has helped me and many others transform our lives. As I said previously, I have written the book I need myself, and never more so perhaps than this and the next chapter.

Because you relied on others for survival, as a child you were acutely sensitive to and could be very frightened by real or imaginary threats of their rejection – for instance when a parent got cross, a teacher expressed disappointment or a group called out some random infringement. You were very small, and parents, teachers and groups seemed very powerful. Because you were so inexperienced at the time, you read what they said or how they behaved as messages about yourself. A small child can't take into account that a parent is under time pressure, a teacher might be having a bad day or that groups are not always right. They don't understand that parents and teachers especially are trying to help them socialize and fit in, so that they can be 'successful' in life. They just hear that they are doing something wrong or are 'less than' in some way. The theory is that, as children, we can take those admonishing and infantilizing voices of authority figures and internalize, generalize, amplify and identify with them to create internal guard rails, psychological mechanisms which warn of the risk of rejection and withdrawal of protection, and try to steer us away from potential danger before it happens, and so spare us shame and pain. These become our inner critics and saboteurs, and their purpose is to protect us and keep us safe. I remember my parents telling me off as a child for screwing up the TV channels with an unfamiliar remote control. Not a big deal, right? But for years afterwards, I internalized their disapproval and believed that I was useless, and so shied away from anything that needed technological skillfulness, be that a job or learning to drive. I *am* useless, I believed, and I need someone else to come and save me – or at least fix a plug and then drive me home. Wired into our brain development in childhood, this negative self-talk affects how confident we feel as adults.

How They Show Up in Our Lives Now

Inner critics and saboteurs are the vestiges of a childhood survival strategy programme, like an old operating system. Think of them as loyal soldiers, fighting a long-ended battle to keep you safe through childhood until you could take care of yourself independently. However, no one has told them that the war is over. That's now your job, and you'll do this in the exercise coming up.

The problem as you try to change your life is that they activate when you move out of your comfort zone to try something new, unknown, challenging or that risks rejection, for instance, dating, saying no to your boss or friends, applying for a new role, starting a new project, going freelance or stepping up in front of people. You may not want them, but try to have compassion for the child you once were. See them as parts of yourself – what psychologists call 'subpersonalities' – that are working to help you cope with such situations. You might think that psychologically speaking there is one of you, and the idea of having many different inner parts or selves runs against this. But think of a time when you had an important task to do, and you struggled with two inner voices, one saying, 'Come on, just get it over with,' and the other, 'But it's a beautiful day outside, don't waste it.' Now you get the idea, and no, it doesn't mean you have multiple personality disorder.

Because inner critics and saboteurs formed when you were young and are frozen in time back in your past, they are still hardwired into your basic survival fear. In short, they act as if you are still five years old and can't distinguish between feeling psychologically vulnerable and being in actual physical peril. Remember in Chapter Two I said your inner sympathetic nervous system alarm can be set off by imagined as much as real danger? Because of this, inner critics shout loud to get your attention – 'You don't know what you're doing and everyone's going to know you're a loser!' – rather than advise in a more adult way – 'Hey, this is new, and you can do it, but don't wing it, prepare.'

Saboteurs also still think you are five and so regress to childlike powerlessness when you feel vulnerable. For instance, they'll say, 'Why do *I* have to change my life? Why doesn't someone else do it for me?' rather than, 'I feel vulnerable right now, but it's okay, I can manage this and still act.' This causes problems when you want to change your life because you need to be able to bear feeling vulnerable when you start creating a new path out of the wood. Inner critics and saboteurs want you to stay there, because its familiarity feels safer, even if it's uncomfortable.

When my client Eva wanted to change her life, she experienced a typical critic attack. She wanted to go from working for a big organization to leading her own events for young women in business. But it felt like riding a horse that refused the first jump, and she wasn't helped by the fact her previous manager had constantly criticized her work and crushed her confidence. The inner-critic mechanism is a track laid in childhood, and as adults we can find it difficult not to internalize and over-identify with the criticism of an authority figure.

As she considered her career shift, her inner critic told her,

'Who are you to do this? Who's going to want to come to one of your sessions? You don't know enough.'

Ouch. Can you hear what's happening? Inner critics sound like the voice of reality because they ventriloquize authority figures. The task is too big, too overwhelming, and you're only five years old – to them anyway. In Eva's case, what do you need to know to run a workshop to help women in business? You need to know a few helpful things about the subject; you need to present them in such a way that people have the opportunity to learn, discuss, practise and reflect; you need to deliver and market them appealingly; and you need to figure out where to do it and what to charge so you can do this sustainably. Her saboteur took one look at the challenge and tempted her into procrastination cul-de-sacs, where she was stuck. But by taking small preparatory steps, Eva would be ready to start, and she would learn more by trying than not. The voices she heard weren't articulating reality but fear. Inner critics and saboteurs alike forget that when you are doing something for the first time, you are on a learning curve. Their demands for instant perfection invite in anxiety and form an obstacle to finding your own path. What a relief to remember you are always a work in progress, always learning, always growing.

I hope you take some comfort from understanding that having inner critics and saboteurs is normal. But this doesn't mean you can allow them to run your life. It also doesn't mean you need to harden and become impervious to fear. Remember what Maria learned: 'It's okay to feel fear, it's not going to kill you.' In fact, accepting your vulnerability is one of the key ways you can demobilize the troops and lessen their power. When Eva realized she was scared, she became a bit easier on herself because it was understandable. She could manage her fear with self-care, preparation, small steps and perspective, and this helped her start.

Spotting Your Inner Critics and Saboteurs

Inner critics and saboteurs will grab for the wheel of your life as you hover between the comfort zone of your old path and the growing zone of your next. You need a better relationship with them so that you can put your wiser self in the driver's seat.

First, you need to spot them – as you did with scripts and 'shoulds' earlier in this book. These are all examples of phrases I have caught clients saying which tell me there's a critic or saboteur in the room. Perhaps you recognize some of these as things you say sometimes. You'd be only human if you did.

'I know this sounds silly, but . . .'

'I am pathetic . . .'

'Why is this happening to me?'

'Can you tell me what to do?'

Once you have spotted one, then it's important to separate yourself from them, as you started to do with the 'shoulds' and scripts. Psychological studies show that when you have more distance from your inner voice, you gain more perspective and leadership over yourself. Say to yourself, 'My inner critic is giving me a hard time today,' or, 'My saboteur is in the room.' You can separate from them even more effectively by giving them a name. You may well have more than one (I certainly do), each with their own distinct way of attacking or undermining you. This also makes them easier to spot in future – remember, they may be a *part* of you but they are not *all* of you; and when you spot them, it's worth remembering that they are powered by fear. Being an adult doesn't mean you don't feel fear, but it helps to check whether your fears are grounded in reality or not, and manage them enough that they don't dictate your life. Here's an introduction to inner critic and saboteur family members my clients and I have identified to help you do this.

The Inner Critic Family

Think about a situation in which you criticize yourself. Tune in to your body as there might be a feeling that accompanies this, such as a tightness in your chest. These techniques can help to take the edge of your stress so you can turn to face your inner critics and saboteurs:

Suggested Practices

- Gently breathe into any sensations in the body, imagining you could soften the space around them.
- 4–4–4 breath (breathe in for a count of four, filling your lungs and expanding your belly, hold for four and breathe out slowly for four).
- Use the Centering and Six Directions Breathing practices from Chapter Two.
- The 'Hello, Goodbye' Practice for Letting Go from Chapter Five is also helpful.

Write down what helps you so you can use it again.

When you are ready, notice if there is a script playing in your head. I know that whenever I sit down to write or when I walk into a room of people I don't know, my inner Shamer and Mind Reader tag-team each other, telling me I am not good enough and everyone will think I am weird and boring. You'll recognize critics by their harsh inner voices and their typical scripts. It may sound strange, but I am going to ask you to welcome them in and become curious and even compassionate, rather than shy away. You might not want to have them, but here they are. Below, you'll find a list of critics and their typical judgements that my clients and I have noticed. You can use any of them to name yours, or choose another name that feels right for you. My clients' examples include the Moaning Meany and Mr Eliot (after a particularly cutting teacher). What matters is that it works for you.

The Shamer: You're not good enough.
The Perfectionist: To be worthy you must be perfect.
The Comparison Maker: Others are better than you.
The Doubter: You can't do this.
The Mind Reader: Everyone will think . . .
The Imposter Buster: You'll be exposed as a fraud.
The Tall Poppy Trimmer: You're getting too big for your boots.
The Tough Guy: Fear is weakness. You need to toughen up.

The Saboteur Family

The inner critic branch of the family has some cousins. Saboteurs may not sound like harsh inner critics when you tune into their voices but they can get in your way when you are trying to do something challenging or out of your comfort zone by disempowering you. Because they are more insidious and slippery, you might not be able to hear them as clearly as the critics, but if you notice that you're avoiding taking action or responsibility for your life, you might be seeing their effects. Again, you can use any of the names below, or come up with your own. A client has one he calls the Joker – a saboteur that cracks a joke to avoid the vulnerability of connection. It's like an invisible puppet master is pulling your strings to veer you away from vulnerability, when sometimes the only way is through.

The Escape Artist: This is hard and I feel anxious about it, so I'll find ways to escape or avoid the task and/or my anxiety, maybe by procrastinating and doing something easier and more pleasurable, keeping busy or 'rescuing' others instead.

The People Pleaser: To be accepted, I need to make others happy.

The Performer: To be accepted, I will only show the world my shiny side.

The Victim: Everyone and everything is against me, and it's too hard.

The Good Girl/Boy/One: I am the decent one; it's everyone else that's the problem.

The Martyr: I will suffer, because I am the better person for doing so.

The Manipulator: If I ask for what I truly want or need, I will be rejected, and so I will be indirect.

The Guard: I am not safe and anyone can hurt me, so I'll expect trouble and disappointment.

Go easy on yourself. It's tempting to double down – to criticize yourself for having inner critics and saboteurs. Then – if you are like me – because you feel bad about yourself, your saboteurs might rush in to rescue you, followed by your critic attacking you for avoiding the issue, retriggering feelings of worthlessness, and the vicious cycle repeats. I am going to give you a self-compassion practice later, which will help, but for now, remember it's normal to have them and you are not alone.

How to Lessen Their Power

Critics and saboteurs are on autopilot, so you don't even notice when they grab the wheel. When you spot one is lurking, take out your journal and write them a letter to help you take back your power. If it feels strange to do this at first, that's understandable. Look at a spot or chair near you and imagine a critic or saboteur sitting there. Writing a letter helps you separate yourself from them, and also slows down your thoughts, which can come in a rush when they grab the wheel. Do your best and note how you feel afterwards. It gets easier with practice.

Exercise: Writing a Letter to an Inner Critic or Saboteur

Here's how to start – you are welcome to use your own words:

Dear [*name of critic or saboteur*],

I hear you. I know you're trying to keep me safe, but I am an adult and so I don't need your services any more.

Is there something you're worried about and would like me to be aware of? How are you trying to protect me?

If you can calm down a little, then I can see if what you're worried about needs my attention. But that doesn't mean anything you say is right. I know you are energized by fear, and sometimes that means you blow things out of proportion and lose perspective.

I hear you are worried about . . . Is this totally true? Is there another way to see this? Who or what might help?

Here's what I want you to know . . . [*I have added suggestions below for ways you might write back to your critics or saboteurs from a more calm, mature, wiser part of you.*]

You can continue your letter any way you want. Make sure that you end it by signing off with, 'Thank you and goodbye.' It might feel odd to say thanks when you might just want to tell them to eff off. But remember they are parts of you, formed when you were a frightened child, so have a little compassion.

Notice how you feel at the end of this exercise.

Here are some ideas of what you might write back to your critics or saboteurs. You don't have to use these exact words; it's more important you find the right ones for you:

Inner Critics

The Shamer: I am worthy.
The Perfectionist: I am/this is good enough.
The Comparison Maker: Others struggle too. They may appear more . . . or less . . . than me in some ways, but this isn't a reflection of reality, or my abilities, or my capacity to learn and grow. I can be inspired by them.

The Doubter: I don't know unless I try.

The Mind Reader: I don't actually have extrasensory perception and know what people think. I may be putting my own fears into their mouths. They might be supportive, and if not, I can find people who are.

The Imposter Buster: People value me for a reason. They might be seeing potential I can't. If I don't know something, I can learn.

The Tall Poppy Trimmer: I can't live my life to make others happy. When I shine, I give others permission to do the same.

The Tough Guy: Feeling vulnerable is normal and understandable.

Saboteurs

The Escape Artist: I'll pay attention to what it is I am trying to avoid and take small steps to address it.

The People Pleaser: I am not responsible for the happiness of others, and I don't have to sacrifice my own. Others want me to be happy.

The Performer: I accept myself for who I am – all of me – and others can too.

The Victim: I am not helpless.

The Good Girl/Boy/One: Everyone has their struggles. I am not perfect either, and I don't need to be.

The Martyr: I don't need to suffer.

The Manipulator: When I ask for what I need, people have a chance to truly know and support me.

The Guard: I am safe. I'll be able to manage. Others can be helpful, and if they can't, it's more a reflection of their capacity than my worthiness.

I write a letter to my critics and saboteurs whenever I notice I am stressed and overwhelmed, or when I am avoiding something, and I suggest you get into the practice as well. It only takes a few minutes and will give you a little more space to make choices with your own hands on the wheel.

You can also take pre-emptive action. Our critics and saboteurs show up more at some times than others, which is why it's helpful to cultivate an inner environment that makes it less easy for them to thrive.

Cultivate Your Inner Environment

Critics and saboteurs are more likely to show up when you are stressed. When you try to find your own path, you are walking into the perfect habitat for them because they feed on uncertainty. In addition, if any of your energy wells are running low, critics and saboteurs are more likely to come and dance in the empty space.

Twelve-step programmes such as Alcoholics Anonymous have an acronym – H.A.L.T. (Hungry, Angry, Lonely, Tired) – which helps addicts notice when their inner state can tip them into the danger zone and make them more likely to reach for the bottle or call their dealer, for instance. It's worth knowing your own personal danger zones for critics and saboteurs.

Journal Questions

Take your journal and create a checklist and personal self-care plan to cultivate an inner environment less favourable to negative inner voices. Ask yourself the following:

- What are the perfect conditions for my inner critics and saboteurs to thrive in?
- What can I do to lessen the likelihood of these conditions arising?
- How can I take care of myself when they do?

Here are the inner environments that feed my inner critics and saboteurs:

- When I haven't meditated or exercised.
- When I haven't had meaningful connection with people and nature for a few days.
- Before my first cup of tea.
- When I am with people I don't know.
- When I am stressed about money, deadlines or a challenge.
- When I feel unsure about the future.
- When I read lots of troubling news or get sucked into an internet rabbit hole.

The good news is that you already have an idea of what

replenishes your wells and have ways to cultivate your own inner environment so those inner critics and saboteurs have less chance to thrive. Even so, don't forget that it's normal for them to show up on speed dial when you are changing your life, so it also helps to have some good self-care strategies in your emotional first-aid kit for when they do. One of the very best is practising self-compassion.

Self-compassion

One of the paradoxes I encounter as a coach is the need to accept ourselves as we are at the same time as wanting to grow and develop. But I think the paradox arises when you misunderstand the relationship between them. They are not pulling in opposite directions. Self-acceptance is accepting your whole self, including your flaws, fears and vulnerability – yes, even your critics and saboteurs. It isn't soft or nice-to-have but a vital resource. Think of a seed. For it to grow and flourish, it has to have good roots. The flower can't bloom without them. Your roots are your capacity to accept and care for yourself. When I accept myself as I am and stop being so hard on myself, I replenish the capacity to affect my life in many ways.

The practice of self-acceptance is compassion. There is some misunderstanding about self-compassion. Here are some of the myths I have heard over the years:

- If I am kind to myself, I'll turn into a blob who never does anything challenging. I'll lose my edge.

- It's self-indulgent or selfish.
- It means letting myself off the hook.

Self-compassion is being kind and understanding to yourself rather than critical or judgemental, and seeing that we are all the same – all imperfect, all capable of making mistakes and failing at times. It's part of our shared humanity, and knowing this can help us feel more connected to each other, and more compassionate towards others too. There's also an active part to self-compassion – wanting to alleviate suffering. Research shows that increasing our capacity for self-compassion reduces stress, anxiety, rumination and fear of failure, and increases our psychological well-being, as well as our motivation and resilience. So much for a soft skill. If you are interested in learning more, then I wholeheartedly recommend the work of Kristen Neff.

My client Pratam was typically hard on himself. Whenever we would start to talk about finding his own path, he felt a tight, thick band compress around his chest that accompanied his inner Imposter Buster critic, fed by his experiences as often the only man of colour in his work environment. This has a potent effect. Self-compassion alone won't solve systemic prejudice, but it can help with the resulting stress, and give people space to make decisions that affect their lives. I suggested to him that we do the exercise below. He winced a little. Like many of us, he found it easier to be compassionate towards others than himself. When he lifted his face after doing it, something had shifted. It was difficult at first, he told me, and then it was as if his heart opened. Now he felt more positive about what he wanted to do and had more ideas about how to do it – or at least how to create more space for it. We are harder on ourselves than we need to be and, rather than helping us, it actually closes down our capacity to find our own path.

Exercise: Practising Self-compassion

1. Close your eyes. Imagine a dear friend who is struggling as you are now. What would you say to them?
2. Write it down in your journal. If you feel stuck, start with, 'I know all your imperfections and vulnerabilities; I accept and love you and know that you are doing your best.'
3. Notice how you feel.

I practise this regularly, especially when I am stressed. It takes things off the boil and gives me more inner space. It can stir up the silt on the riverbed of your emotions, so be gentle with yourself. The centering practices from Chapter Two, especially Six Directions Breathing or the 'Hello, Goodbye' practice from Chapter Five help you experience difficult emotions, process them a little, and reconnect with your Big I self, which can hold them without being overwhelmed by them.

Self-compassion is a wise practice in the swampy transition as your find your path, and a foundation for it when you do. You don't need to be born with it; you can develop it. Research shows that the more you practise self-compassion, the more you retrain your inner pathways. When you notice you are being hard on yourself, you can choose to change your self-talk, and through regular practice feel its deeper effects on your life as your brain rewires from criticism to compassion. You can take back the wheel.

Self-acceptance is one of the cornerstones of a more meaningful life. I have discovered through doing this work that what I thought were vulnerabilities are, in fact, gifts. Now I can connect with people at a deeper, more empathetic level.

But there is more. Remember, you're bigger on the inside, and within you, ready to be uncovered, are your inner allies ready to help you find your own path. Your inner critics and saboteurs are on speed dial, and although you have wiser inner voices, you may have lost their number, or they get drowned out by the robustness of the others. You are ready to make a choice that will change your life and take it out into the world to find the outer allies who are going to be your support team.

8. Find Allies

Here's a story I feel vulnerable about telling you. The week before I submitted this book to my publisher, I was seized with overwhelming anxiety. I had been writing on my own for months and suddenly became aware that I was about to let it go. I thought of all the ways I had failed to do a good job and all the criticism I had coming. I felt sick to my stomach at the prospect of being pub- licly exposed – what had I done? My inner critics threw me around like a rag doll in a dog's mouth, telling me I didn't know enough (the Shamer was in session), people would think it was bad (the Mind Reader close behind), I would be unmasked as a fraud (the fiendish facepalm of the Imposter Buster) – and that meant I was in essence a bad person. I feared I had been swept away by my own arrogance and would pay a terrible price. The saboteurs told me it was too hard for me to write a book and that I should call my editor the next day to tell her I wanted to forget the whole thing. I felt so ashamed. Long hours passed. It was the middle of the night, I couldn't call a friend for help. But I found one within myself.

In a version of a folktale attributed to the Cherokee and Lenape peoples of North America, two wolves live close to a camp. One is a vicious beast that would rip out your throat and carry away your children given half a chance. The other is a strong, proud creature that can protect the camp from predators. In a fight, which one wins? The answer is the one you feed. When you feed critics and saboteurs, they take the wheel of your life and sabotage your journey across the threshold – as mine were trying to that night. They were trying to keep me hidden safe in my comfort zone. But if, on our own journeys, we let them take them the wheel, we don't step forward into the new challenges we'll meet when we try to find our own path, and I would not have written this book if I had let them take charge. Even though I coach people on this, I often have my own critics and saboteurs on speed dial – as might you. It's normal and understandable. But there is help at hand, and I called on it that night.

In the last exercise in the previous chapter, you fed your own compassionate, positive inner voice, and directed it towards yourself. It's always in you, though it can sometimes be difficult to hear through the noise of the critics. Sometimes I haven't wanted to let my critics go because I felt I needed them to motivate myself. However, research shows that a compassionate and supportive inner voice is a far more effective motivator than a harsh and critical one. When I trained as a coach with the Co-Active Training Institute, they had a wonderful concept they called the Inner Leader, and when I practised meditation, self-compassion and the reparenting technique I include below, I learned more about how to feed a positive voice to nurture the part of me that feels vulnerable, and how powerful it can be – it's a game changer for me and for my clients. You can also see it simply as your Big I self, knowing you, loving you, championing you and wanting the best for you, seeing the big picture beyond all the distractions and busyness of Little I life, inner critic judgements and saboteur avoidances. It's the part of you that wants you to find your own path and is there with you every step of the way.

Just as you can have a number of different inner critics and saboteurs, you can also have different positive inner voices, parts of you that are kind to a friend for instance, or internalized from or inspired by people you know or admire – a friend, relative, coach, teacher or public figure. When I was younger, my friends and I had a mantra whenever we felt troubled – what would Madonna say? You can also draw them from archetypes, such as the hero, the wise one, the explorer or the caregiver, or even from nature in the form of an animal, tree or river. The idea here is to nurture the positive inner voices that can help you as an adult. You'll meet mine later.

I am going to give you two techniques that I use for myself and with clients, so you can find your inner allies when you need them. Later in this chapter, you're going to start to build and nurture relationships with outer allies, who will support you as you find and walk your path. My inner ally helped me through that night; one of my outer allies was there for me the next morning.

Soothe Your Inner Child

Each of us has an Inner Child – a part of ourselves that sometimes feels frightened and overwhelmed. Finding your own path is going to cause you to feel vulnerable – and that's exactly what you want to feel, as it shows you are really making change, rather than just rearranging the furniture of your life, though it can be uncomfortable or even painful to experience. My Inner Child felt vulnerable about writing this book, and I needed to be able to take care of it in a healthy way, through what psychotherapists call *reparenting*, without giving it the steering wheel of my life. Children tend not to be the best drivers, after all. As adults, we can sometimes feel a bit resistant to the idea that we have an Inner Child – as if that means we are immature in some way. Think of your Inner Child as the part of yourself that feels vulnerable at times. Don't brush it away or hide it under a lid of shame. Give it some grown-up care, and as you do, you'll discover an inner part of yourself that will be a great ally.

I'd like to you meet my client Dalia. Dalia is a lovely woman. Everybody likes her. She thinks of others, has integrity, warmth and empathy, and delivers great results to her company. She tells me she knows that having a new boss means things are chaotic, and that she'll be working late nights until the ship steadies. She understands why her friends went out last night for drinks and didn't invite her. After all, she's never available these days. She wants change in her life, it's just that things are a bit busy at the moment. It will get easier in a month. Maybe six. But there it is, that little dance I notice around the edge of her face, a flutter of excess energy as if something very small is waving wildly. I ask if she notices it too. For the first time since our session started, she stops talking and pauses. She cocks her head as if straining to listen, then catches it, and takes a very deep breath as the newly freed message from herself to herself finally bursts into consciousness.

Dalia is furious. Her face flushes with more aliveness than I have seen in our coaching session so far. Her eyes fill with tears and she starts batting them away, as the part of her that fears losing control grabs for the wheel.

Here's the critical point. In this precious moment, she has a choice. She can let her inner critic harangue her for being a crybaby, and pull back the tears, returning them to the inner reservoir which lies locked under the twin guards of shame and guilt. She can give the saboteur the wheel, cracking a joke, changing the subject, continuing to pretend it doesn't matter. Or she can stay with that part of her that wants to speak, the part that's vulnerable but that has the power to open a gateway to real change.

I watch as a tear wobbles along her lower eyelid. She frowns, and then something arrives with new, tender clarity: 'It hurts,' she whispers.

In my job, I am always deeply moved when I witness tiny acts of courage, such as when a person chooses to stay with vulnerability, no matter how uncomfortable, rather than putting on their habitual game face. Lovely, decent, furious, hurt Dalia has built a tremulous bridge to her inner self, which at this moment is as fragile as the surface tension shaping those tears. Now she can learn tools to strengthen it so she can access its truth, wisdom and compassion for the rest of her life. For Dalia, for us all, what's crucial is the type of attention we give our Inner Child.

Here's an image that may help you to picture it. Imagine a small child standing at the edge of a swimming pool for the first time – frightened and hesitant. I remember my first swimming lesson: I had armbands, a ring around my waist and gripped two floats so tightly my fingertips left dents in the polystyrene as I inched, terrified, towards the water. Now imagine that a critic and a saboteur walk up to the child.

The Tough Guy believes that vulnerability is weakness and you just have to get over it. A classic inner critic, in other words. I have witnessed so many people rain down a blitzkrieg of self-criticism upon themselves for feeling vulnerable: 'I am so stupid/pathetic/childish.' A shove might get you in the pool but the shame might eventually pull you under if you rely on it to motivate you.

The Escape Artist. Compared to the Tough Guy, this saboteur can feel like a blessed relief. What does it feel like for that inner vulnerable child to be 'rescued', with promises they will never again be made to do anything that scares them, and stopping tears and fears with offers of sweet distractions and avoidance? To be honest, there are times when I welcome this one myself. But once I have watched every episode of *Star Trek* ever made, eaten bags of crisps the size of my head and generally given myself a free pass, I am still at the edge of the pool. If I can manage my fear and get in the water, the world might open up before me. If I listened to the Escape Artist, I would never learn to manage fear, and I wouldn't know that I could. That knowledge is the sweet gift of experience and the bedrock of true confidence: the kind that emerges from knowing that whatever happens you can take action and recover from any struggles and setbacks in a way that can give life meaning.

The Good Parent. This inner ally doesn't push or shame, indulge or avoid, but comes alongside that trembling Inner Child and says, 'I hear you're afraid, and I get it. It's scary stuff. But I am going to stay with you. I am not going to abandon you. I am an adult who can take care of you, and we're going to do this together.' Can you feel the difference?

Rather than rejecting yourself for being afraid, or avoiding fear, as critics and saboteurs do, what if you compassionately acknowledged that part of you that's afraid? When you stand next to your own Inner Child, listening, responding with compassion and offering adult support, you find a way through being overwhelmed by fear, hurt and vulnerability.

Whenever you notice the inner critics and saboteurs have you in their clutches, reparent your Inner Child with these Five As.

Exercise: Reparenting with the Five As

1. Think of something you feel vulnerable about, perhaps a difficult choice you have to make, a conversation you need to have or a challenge you need to face.

2. Sometimes it can help to imagine that Inner Child part of yourself next to you, or, if it feels safe to do so, focus on the part of your body that feels the emotion most intensely. Ask that part of you, tenderly and with care, 'How do you feel?' and let it speak. It helps to write this down in your journal.

3. Now speak back to your Inner Child using the Five As in this order:

> *Acknowledge*: 'I hear you. I know you are hurt/ frightened/vulnerable.'
>
> *Accept*: 'That's understandable.'
>
> *Assure*: 'It's okay. I am not going to abandon you.'
>
> *Ask*: 'What do you need?' Listen to anything that comes up. It might be to feel safe, to talk with a friend, or to rest.
>
> *Aid*: 'We'll do this together. I am an adult, and we'll find a way through.'

Whenever I feel hurt, angry or frightened, I practise this. I have a strong fear of abandonment, and it helps to remind my Inner Child – the part of me that is scared, the little girl whose mum passed away – that I won't abandon her/myself. When you cultivate your own Good Parent inner voice, you build that bridge to your wise, compassionate, adult self.

Dalia blinks. Once she spoke back to that hurt and vulnerable part of herself as a good parent would, she could identify what she needed.

'I need to assert boundaries. To listen to that inner voice that tells me when it's too much, and to give myself time and space to figure out my plan.'

Now she has the action to start to change her life and the adult confidence to support herself. Every day Dalia does her best to be there for her young daughter. She hadn't realized she also needed that unconditional kindness and those skills of listening, support, reassurance and encouragement for herself. She has been there for everyone else, but not herself, and now this is going to change. It's a deep and profound shift.

Connecting with Inner Allies

Just as there are different inner critics and saboteurs, you can have a whole family of inner allies if you want. The list below is one that includes many that I use, as well as some my clients have created for themselves. Pick those that might help you most. I encourage you to add your own and will give you a few further suggestions in the exercise below.

The Inner Ally Family

The Compassionate Friend: who supports you as you would support another.
The Inner Coach: who believes in you and encourages you to take action.
The Curious One: who takes an interest in what's really going on under the surface.

The Mountaineer: who, rather than being overwhelmed when they look at the task ahead, gathers what they need and takes the first step.

The Explorer: who courageously embraces an opportunity for adventure.

The Seer: who wisely rises above the day-to-day details to see the longer-term perspective and clarifies what's really important.

The Storyteller: who reminds you of everything you have already overcome.

The Inner Buddha: whether you count yourself as spiritual or not, the image of the Buddha in a state of peace with everything is an example of the potential we all have within us.

You can have as many allies as you need. Remember you can base them on people you know or public figures. One client chose her grandmother. When I feel prickles of insecurity about ageing, I imagine what Helen Mirren would say, and her response always includes a vivacity for life and some juicy language. For now, choose whoever would be most helpful to you at this moment and pick up your journal again. Your ally has a message for you.

Exercise: A Letter from Your Inner Ally

1. Close your eyes. Take a few deep breaths. As you breathe out, have gratitude for your life and this moment.

2. Bring to mind the inner ally you need. It can be:

- From the list above.
- Someone you know, like a dear friend, a kind relative or a teacher who encouraged you.
- Someone you don't know but admire.
- An animal, perhaps a much-loved pet or a creature that has some meaning for you or that you like, such as a deer, eagle or horse.
- A figure or image from your imagination. Some people imagine a ball of light, for example.
- A place or object in nature. I have a favourite tree in the woods near where I live that I use as an ally – a great beech with spreading branches that offers shelter and a long perspective on what really matters. You might have a mountain, beach, river or flower that is special to you.

3. What qualities does your inner ally possess that you need right now? Write them down. It could be living for the moment, truth, bravery, wisdom, power, kindness, playfulness, self-belief, humour – whatever you need.

4. Now, in your journal, write yourself a letter from the perspective of this inner ally, starting with: 'Dear [*your name*], Remember that I love you and see the goodness in you.' What message do they have for you? What do they want you to know? You can reread these letters if you find yourself struggling or need to connect with your allies in future.

5. End the letter with: 'I'll always be there for you, love, [*name of ally*].'
6. Notice how you feel.

Check in with your ally or allies daily, and whenever you have a choice to make.

On the night of my anxiety attack, I shakily wrote myself a letter from one of my allies – I imagine an old wise woman. When I feel overwhelmed, scared or not sure what to do or be, her letters always give me support. Sometimes she tells me to persevere, sometimes to rest. Sometimes she tells me to go for a walk and notice signs and lessons from nature. Sometimes she suggests I take a break and make a cup of tea, and that is enough. When I start writing a letter from her, I never know what's she's going to say to me, but somehow, in between starting and finishing it, she arrives and tells exactly me what I need to hear. That night, this is what she said:

It's understandable you feel frightened. You're about to let go of control over the book. Whatever happens, remember, even if the book is bad, even if the reviews are bad, you are not bad. Your essence is good. Writing a book is a brave thing to do. Try to rest until morning, and then make that cup of tea and take a look again at what you have written, to see if there are changes you need to make before you give it to your editor. You can still do that. Breathe. Whatever happens, you'll be okay. You have this.

I still had a restless night. But I also had a way forward and a helpful perspective, so my fear didn't paralyse me or cause me to do something rash. Like you, I am in the boat, digging my oar into the river, shaking like a leaf at times, but I am much better at supporting myself now than I was a few years ago.

Here are some of my clients' inner allies. Graham, who wanted to step back from his life's work to create a full and rich retirement but who always gave too much to others and not enough to himself, received unconditional love from his loyal, faithful and friendly dog. Pratam, who wanted to put more of his time into creativity, wrote a letter to himself from Yoda from the *Star Wars* films, who gave him some good coaching. Maria, who needed strength to start a new career outside of academia and to leave her partner, received a letter from her beloved mother and brother, who had passed away. She kept them with her by imagining them in the form of two tall trees by the stream outside her new home, enfolding her in their arms and supporting her. Their letter reminded her of past generations of her ancestors.

You are bigger on the inside. By this point in the book, I hope you're realizing this and starting to explore the benefits of having a better relationship with more of yourself – your values, purpose, wells of energy, inner critics and saboteurs, and inner allies. It's like meeting yourself anew. It's part of the process of finding your own path.

Before I leave the subject of allies, I want to take a look at the kind that you find in the outer world.

Your Outer Allies

You need to find your outer as well as your inner tribe. You also may need to draw boundaries in some way with people who – for whatever reasons – may try to keep you in your old life. This doesn't mean you have to ditch your family and current friends because they are in some way bad people. This isn't about judgement of them as people but discernment of what you need now. Discernment is saying, 'I love you, but right now your input isn't helpful as I try to find my own path, so I need to create some boundaries.'

When I was trying to shift my life, family and some friends expressed concern: 'Are you sure? How are you going to make a living? Why would you give up a salaried job? There are too many life coaches already, you'll never find clients.' Others said, 'You're no fun now,' or even, 'I don't know who you are any more.' It's hard hearing this. It's as if your inner critics and saboteurs jumped out of your head and became flesh. It feels as if you have to risk rejection to become the person you are ready to be. Truth is, sometimes you do.

I advise people seeking their own path to take a look at the people with whom they spend most time. Reduce the impact of those who, for whatever reason, will keep you from finding your own path, drawing internal boundaries. For instance:

- They mean well, but what works for them doesn't work for me.

- They worry about the unknown and don't want me to put myself in jeopardy. I value their love, and I am not rejecting them if I choose to find my own path.
- Their anxieties reflect who they are, not who I am.
- I do not have to live my life to please them.

Let's get clear on what you do need from people. You need people who positively reflect back your strength, capability and potential, and who believe in you – in other words, your outer allies. My own outer allies were friends and colleagues who said, 'You'd be great at that.' They don't need to kiss your backside; they can challenge you in healthy ways that help you grow. One of my friends told me I needed to quit hiding and write. Quite often, they have similar values to your own. When I met my friend the morning after my anxiety attack, she reminded me of my courage. When I felt as if I had failed, she reminded me how far I had come. She also offered me practical help and support, putting me in touch with someone and recommending a stress-reducing walk.

Outer allies can also inspire you by their own example. Here's what happened to Maria, the unhappy American academic. When she was stuck, her friend Elizabeth took her for lunch, and that conversation changed her life.

'I had to go back to a job I hated, and I couldn't do that any more. I was also in a bad financial situation, which made me feel even more depressed. We were in a booth in a restaurant and she said, "Well, okay, so what do you want to do?" She used to tell me about her work as a psychologist in her second act. She went back to study in her thirties after being a secretary. When she asked that question, it was the first moment I had ever thought about it. And I said, "I want to do what you do. I want to talk to people, and understand and help them." It was one of those crystal-clear moments. Then she asked, "How will you do that?" I said I didn't know and she said, "Well, research it." And I did. And one action led to the next.'

What also helps is having a community of people going through the same thing, finding their own way to a meaningful life. You can feel isolated when you are stressed, but you are not alone. As Maria said, when she was going through her divorce, having friends in the same boat helped: 'I felt that I wasn't alone in this scary thing, that we were all trying to figure out what we do.'

Having community has huge benefits to our health and well-being. How do we go about finding ours? Our current friends, acquaintances and the internet are great places to start. Whether online or in real life, put 'have meaningful connections' above the 'Important' line on your weekly To-do List. Here are some ideas:

- Men's, women's and non-binary groups or circles are great, intentional spaces to share and not be judged.
- If you can, take an online course. People who learn together can form great tribes.
- Make investments. In our busy lives, it has become too easy to lose contact with friends.

Make a commitment to connect or reconnect with people. It takes about one hundred hours of time spent together for people to form a friendship, and it is an investment well worth making. It doesn't cost anything.

- Ask. Perhaps there is someone you met but never followed up with. Ask them if they'd like to connect. The worst that will happen is they say no.
- We can all have a tendency to go to work, the gym, church or any other space, do what we came to do and leave in quite a transactional way. Perhaps there is someone there you might suggest meeting up with.
- Be intentional. Suggest a gathering somewhere, such as a park or café.

Accountability Partners

When I teach a course, I place people into pods, or communities of support, which they often continue long after the course has finished. I recommend you have an accountability partner or pod (with no more than four members). People are 95 per cent likely to meet a goal when they build in ongoing meetings with partners or pods to check in on their progress. You'll need some clear agreements to make sure you don't spend your time chatting. I had an accountability partner when I was shifting my life to coaching – a friend who wanted to make her first film – and this is the contract we drew up together. Please adapt the agreement below to what works for all of you.

Accountability Partner or Pod Contract

- We agree to connect every week/fortnight/ month for between thirty minutes and an hour. (Short, focused and regular is best.)
- We also agree to connect through text or online in between meet-ups between the hours of x and x.
- We give ourselves x number of minutes at the beginning for a quick hello. Then we get down to work.
- Our time is split equally between us. We honour each other's time and end our slot punctually. Each segment is focused on each person in turn exclusively.
- During our slot, we will talk about our progress.
- We offer support with permission, reminding ourselves that sometimes what works for us might not work for another. We don't interrupt.
- No one is allowed to skip their slot. Even if we haven't done anything, we talk about what got in the way and commit to action before next time. We can also ask for support.
- We end by committing to action.
- Next time we connect, we agree to start our segment with an update on progress, end with a commitment to next steps, and agree how others can hold us accountable.

Done well, this will supercharge your progress. You might like to work through some of the exercises in this book together. A couple of friends and I – all working in the same field – have an ongoing commitment to connect every few weeks to check in, share and listen. I can't tell you how nourishing and supportive this is.

I know that when you feel lost, vulnerable or stuck, it can feel as if you are the only person who feels this way – as if everyone else is at a party to which you haven't been invited. It's not true, of course; everyone struggles at some point in their lives. It's part of the deal called being human. When you step out of the woods to find your own path, you may have to face internal and external obstacles, and having inner and outer support helps. I can't tell you that on your path you'll live a life free from inner critics or saboteurs, because that's never been a destination at which I have arrived. I can't tell you that everyone you know is going to support you. But, as I have found, with your own inner positive voice and with a tribe who support and encourage you, you'll be more able to be a little bit wiser, kinder and courageous, and that will make all the difference, especially as you start to take action, which is where we are going next on this journey.

9. Give Yourself Permission to Make Choices

If I was sitting with you right now, I'd ask you how you are doing. This is deep work – especially the last two chapters, as you met and worked with inner critics, saboteurs and allies at an emotional level, in the places you feel vulnerable and where you haven't always been kind to yourself. After doing this work with clients, I always recommend some self-care. I suggest you put the kettle on, or go for a walk, and keep reminding yourself of the courage it takes to find your own path.

Whatever brings you to the threshold to create a more meaningful life, at some point you will yearn for solid ground under your feet again. You can feel impatient to make decisions. But they need to be informed by all the work you have done so far, lest you exchange a frying pan for a fire. I see the problems that can happen when people rush into a new chapter of their lives without doing the inner work, without a clear idea of what to move towards for a fulfilling life or ways to manage and replenish energy, tackle obstacles and support themselves. Because of the work you have done so far, you may already be noticing changes in how you think, feel and act, and how the world around you responds. In this chapter, you'll practise a great way to come up with options, and decide which ones are seeds for your new path. In the following chapter, I'll share the next stage in the process to nurture your seed ideas into action and test them. This is where your inner work hits the road.

Sometimes, however, between reflection and taking action, an 'edge' can appear – you'll sense it when you start to feel nervous or want to avoid or resist it. That's okay, it is normal. Knowing the changes you want to make in your life is not enough without permission to act. I don't mean waiting for someone else's permission but giving it to yourself. Whenever I reach the jump-off point of making decisions and taking action, the editors, auditors, doubters and doomsayers lie in wait, sharpening their critical tools. Saboteurs set up camp with ways to avoid deciding or doing. Once you have the wheel back in your hands, using practices from the previous two chapters, you need to give yourself permission to turn it and move forward. Then you can pull ahead of analysis-paralysis and perfectionism by generating, germinating, nurturing and testing your options with useful scrutiny.

Giving Yourself Permission

You met Graham in Chapter One. He wanted to let go of running his business day-to-day and live the next part of his life for himself. However, he wasn't giving himself full permission to think or say what his heart truly desired – 'I need'. He's not alone. Often I think that my job as a coach is to give people permission to do what they know deep down they want. In Chapter Five, you explored how awareness of mortality can be a great impetus to living your fullest life. It gives you permission to live your life for you – not for others or for all those 'shoulds' and scripts. I have found that when I gave myself permission, some people didn't like it but others celebrated it, so happy that I was finally there – present and more available to them *because* I was more present to myself, not in spite of that.

Here's the story of a seminal moment when I finally gave myself permission. On my last day of training as a coach with the Co-Active Training Institute, one of the instructors asked for a volunteer to be coached by them in front of the group. I had secretly longed for this throughout my training, but I hadn't put myself out there because I was ashamed of my own desires. I often pretended I didn't want something I really did. It's a pretty sneaky Cool Girl saboteur, which, of course, doesn't actually spare me pain so much as conceal it with a shrug. When someone else was picked, I would force a smile. This time, the instructor asked people to close their eyes, and asked those who hadn't yet been picked, but who wanted to be, to raise their hands. I felt my heart simultaneously open with longing and clench with fear of disappointment. But because no one could see me, I raised my hand. Then I heard my name being called. I opened my eyes. My heart pounded. Everyone was looking at me. I was exposed.

I stood in front of everyone, and the trainer asked me to state publicly what I really wanted for my life. I struggled. She kept pushing me. I came up with something that felt vaguely socially acceptable – not too big, and not very authentic. Like many of you, I have a Tall

Poppy Trimmer critic and cringe when I have to state an ambition or dream, thinking I must sound very full of myself. Occasionally, I still need to have a conversation with it to prise its fingers off the steering wheel. This was going to help now.

The trainer asked me to try again.

'State your dream and give yourself full permission to own it,' she said.

I froze, whilst my inner critics and saboteurs danced. Finally, I said,

'All I have to bring is myself. I know I do this big show, but the truth is that I am vulnerable and frightened. So I know how that feels, and if I can help other people who feel the same, then that is what I have to give.'

I had fixed my eyes on the floor, hoping that no one would be able to see my face. Now I slowly raised them, expecting to see a row of blank, bored faces. Imagine the shock I received when I saw people's eyes shining with joy and tears. One of them spoke, full of emotion,

'Finally. I have been waiting for months to truly see you. Thank you.'

The room erupted with applause. I nearly fell over with astonishment. I had given myself permission to be me, and rather than pushing people away, I had brought them closer. I wasn't diminishing others or inevitably going to be rejected – as my old stories and critics had warned me.

Here's your moment. It's time to give yourself permission to find a meaningful path.

Exercise: Give Yourself Permission

1. Mark a line on the floor or on the ground. Have a friend with you to witness, if that feels right. If movement is not easy for you, take a physical object that represents your new life and set it down within reach in front of you.
2. Say to yourself, 'When I cross that threshold (or take up this object), I am giving myself permission to live my life for me.'
3. Do whatever preparation feels right. You could write down everything you long for. Move, if your body wants to or is able. Breathe deeply. Centre.
4. Stand on one side of the line, or sit in front of your object, and feel your feet, and/or your sitting bones, connected to the earth. Connect with all the people who have your back by imagining a hand there, supporting you. Know as well that your story also supports you – all your life experience.
5. Then take a deep breath and step across the line, or pick your object up. Name your dream out loud, and say, 'I give myself permission to live a more meaningful life.'
6. Breathe deeply again. Notice how you feel. Journal about it.

At the start of this book, I spoke of crossing a threshold. Well, here it is – the threshold that ultimately matters: the permission you give yourself to find your own path.

You met Devon before. He made huge changes in his life by giving himself permission to let go of the things he thought made him happy but didn't, such as his need to achieve and be validated, and to believe that he was worthy, no matter what financial struggles he experienced. The turning point came for him when he gave himself permission to name what he needed, which was a steady paying job to give him security, while using his gifts and experience.

'Within moments of that, the universe was like, "Well, here you are." The phone rang, and it was an agency offering me a job in social care.'

Even if the universe doesn't answer you as immediately and clearly as it did for Devon, by giving yourself permission to name or ask for what you want and need out loud, you'll have a much better chance of achieving it than if you don't. One of the reasons for this is because of what psychologists call *priming*. If you are clear what you are looking for and give yourself permission to do so, you are more likely to see opportunities for it in your life, just as if when you know you want a small family electric car, for instance, you start seeing them everywhere. For the same reason, don't keep it to yourself – tell people. Prime them to help, so they can see opportunities for you. One of the biggest steps I took was giving myself permission to tell people I was now working as a life coach and looking for clients.

Generating Ideas

With compass in hand and permission in heart, along with the rest of the work you have done so far in this book, it's time to generate options. When it comes to changes you want to make in your life, it's a mistake to imagine you must spend months in analysis mode, researching that one perfect activity, location or role. Initially at least, head in the opposite direction: 'go wide' and come up with a few options. Linus Pauling, the Nobel Prize-winning chemist, once said that the way to have good ideas was to have lots of them and then throw out the bad ones. You cross the threshold to thresh out seeds, and a playful decision-making game later in this chapter will help you winnow them.

When I started to work with a coach, we brainstormed ideas. Here's how we did it.

Exercise: Generating Options for a More Meaningful Life

Write down as many ideas as you can come up with for options for your own path: courses, locations, tribes, roles, relationships, activities, projects, dreams or jobs (or anything else you can come up with). Here are some tips:

- Start with your key words or statement. It can be as simple as 'A more meaningful life' or 'My own path'. Include your values, purpose and anything else that helps you from the notes in your journal. I wrote, 'What would help me live my values of Growth, Love, Service and Creativity?'

- Set a time limit of a few minutes. It is amazing what happens when you close down potentially open-ended variables. Some artists use a limited palette or materials to reduce their options and force themselves to be more creative; it also serves to contain overwhelm when faced with a blank canvas.

- Aim for between five and eight options. Even if you don't generate that many, aiming for it will help you come up with more than if you didn't have a target.

- Encourage disruptive, wild and weird outlier ideas. For instance, when I brainstorm with clients, I throw in the option 'join an ashram' – not because it's a viable or desirable option for most people, but it serves two purposes:
  - It knocks them out of the rut of narrow incremental thinking and gives them permission to consider more radical options.
  - Even if joining an ashram isn't an option, there may well be something that gives them a positive or negative feeling about it – which is invaluable data. Some of my clients like the idea of having more community, for instance; others are clear that they don't want to leave home. Every client with whom I have worked has found some useful element in a wildcard.

- Now step away and do something else – housework, cooking, painting, running or walking, for instance. If you prime your mind to come up with ideas, work on it for a bit and then go and do something that doesn't require much thought and doesn't overstimulate you (so no screens), the prefrontal cortex in your brain, which acts as the gatekeeper or inhibitor of your creativity, takes a break and ideas pop up. Which is why you can come up with ideas in the shower or in the supermarket queue. Just make sure you have some way of capturing them, so you don't forget.

Take the pressure off yourself. Remember this is just a draft. Trying to find the 'right' or 'perfect' answer can stress you out, and that blocks you from seeing what's possible. You are just coming up with options here, so don't start editing down or making decisions about them yet.

Here's Jan, whom you met in Chapter Two, struggling to find time to clear her home as her first step to finding her own path. Her options were:

- Take a year out.
- Apply for other jobs (she felt uninspired, ineffective and micromanaged in her current one).
- Volunteer.
- Become a dancer. This was her 'crazy' idea, but it had always been her fantasy as a girl.
- Do more art.
- Join an ashram (of course!).

How to Make Decisions

Once you have some options, select which you'd like to explore further at the moment. It doesn't need to be just one, it can be more, or elements from a few. If you are like me, you can get very into your head here, so I like to play a game to listen to my whole self and tap into the rich reservoir of wisdom and information within me that I can access through my body. That isn't to say our heads are wrong – they are great advisors – but we need to tap into more information. One choice might seem very sensible according to my head (a big-paying contract or a move, for instance), but it doesn't *feel* right – sometimes because it's out of alignment with my values, sometimes because my gut tells me that the offer might not be as great as it seems. What use is the extra money or a new location if it means you don't spend time with the people you love, or you have to work with someone you are not sure you trust? As you go through your options, you're going to use your so-called *triple brain* – head, heart and gut (or intuition) – as well as some other prompts to help shake out information from yourself.

Use Your Head, Heart and Gut

A growing body of knowledge supports the idea that decision-making isn't solely a brain-led process but also involves emotion and intuition, which you feel in your body. The emotion of your heart and the intuition of your gut *together* with the knowledge of your head propels you to action.

Thinking is great, but too much of it can leave you spinning your wheels with analysis-paralysis. Here's how you know if you are in your head:

Analysing – you focus on the details of what is going on and why, without taking action.

Debating – working out pros and cons is important but not enough in itself, and it can lead to endless rumination. There will be pros and cons to any decision; there's rarely any perfect choice that doesn't require work, sacrifice and compromise.

Rationalizing – ever go back and forth justifying a decision to yourself? You're probably overruling your heart and gut.

We need to keep our heads when finding our own path, but we also need to connect with what we care about and what our intuition tells us.

Although we imagine the brain as our only control centre, studies show that the heart actually sends more messages up to the brain than vice versa. When we experience emotions, such as compassion, appreciation and joy, our heart rhythm becomes coherent and harmonious, and we feel more calm, positive and willing to act. The heart really is intimately connected to processing emotions. You'll know you're tuned into your heart when you long for or care strongly for something or someone.

Finally, intuition is that sneaking little voice you sometimes wish you listened to more often. Unlike anxiety, which tends to conjure up numerous possible solutions to imagined future bad-case scenarios, intuition can often lead to a concrete decision or action. It's that feeling in the pit of your stomach you can't explain logically, or a sense of clarity or calm after a tough decision, reassuring you that you've done the right thing.

You hold so much wisdom inside you, and when you tune into head, heart and gut, you can check if you feel truly aligned with a choice or direction. Whenever I need to make a decision, I check in with my triple brain. When all three are in alignment with a 'yes', then I'll know it could be a good choice for me. Let's practise this ready for the decision-making exercise coming up.

Exercise: Head, Heart and Gut Awareness

1. What's a small decision you want to make today or this week? Perhaps what to do this weekend.
2. Bring your attention to your head. Start to tune into your thoughts. What does your head *think* about this? Write it down, starting with 'I think . . .' It might come up with very sensible ideas for catching up on emails, running errands or fulfilling obligations.
3. Now, bring your attention down into your heart-space. What does your heart *want*? Write what you *feel*, starting with 'I long for . . .' Notice if you start to tilt your head, place your hand on it or start with 'I think . . .' Your head just jumped in and grabbed the mike.

Don't beat yourself up – this can take some practice.

4. Bring your attention to your gut. What does it say? When I ask what my gut *senses* about a situation, it responds, 'Yep', 'Nope' or 'Meh', without the analysis or debating of the head or the yearning of the heart. Write down 'My gut feeling is . . .' Sometimes it can take practice as we're often unused to listening to it, so don't worry if it takes a few tries.

If you notice that a part of you isn't aligned, get curious. What's going on? Perhaps your plan sounds very sensible to the head, but your heart isn't in it. Or maybe your gut has picked up on something that doesn't feel right. Your heart and gut may say yes, but your head wants you to pay attention to some potential downsides if you make this choice. On a larger scale, I was once looking to buy a flat and found a place I loved, but my head worked out it would put my finances under considerable strain and imagined what it would feel like every night to lie in bed worrying about money. My heart and gut didn't like this picture at all, so I didn't make an offer. If you notice your head, heart and gut aren't aligned, it doesn't mean you say no, but it's a good idea to slow down and check what the issues are, rather than overruling them. You can't reason your way to find your own path; it takes head-thinking, heart-feeling and gut-sensing. You're now ready to bring this into decision-making.

Exercise: The Decision-making Game

When I first did this exercise with my coach, I stood up and moved, because it shifted energy and got me out of my head. But you can also do it sitting down, if movement isn't easy for you. The aim here is not to find a perfect solution – we're going to explore and play, harvesting important information.

You'll need your journal, some pieces of paper and some space, if you are able to move easily. If not, sit at a table. As you explore your options, journal or record your responses with a voice recorder, or if you have an impartial friend or accountability partner, you can reciprocate: one person does the exercise whilst the other reads the instructions and questions and writes down the responses. Sometimes, when you go back, it's hard to remember accurately. Most of all, have fun!

1. Write each of your ideas from the Options exercise down on separate pieces of paper.
2. Set up your space as you did for the Give Yourself Permission exercise earlier, with a line for you to cross, and keep your options in your hand. Stand on one side of the line. If it's easier, arrange your pieces of paper on a table in front of you and sit where you can see them.
3. If standing, shuffle the pieces of paper and randomly pick one. Put the others down for now. Then cross the line to give yourself permission to consider the option you picked.

You can hold it in your hand, or place it on the floor, walk around it, taking different perspectives on it, and even stand on it. If sitting, pick up a piece of paper. Notice what that option feels like: you might feel excited, or you might feel an aversion. Here's what to do next.

i. Tune into your head, heart and gut, using the practice above. What does each say about this option? Record this in your journal or on a voice recorder, or have your companion write it down for you.

ii. If you notice a 'no', ask yourself, 'Is there an element of this that appeals?'

iii. Check in with an inner ally. Do they have something to say about this option?

iv. Imagine that you made this choice. How would you feel six months or a year later? Sometimes I meet people who tell me they would love to write a book. They often imagine reading glowing reviews. I ask them to imagine being alone at their computer for months.

4. Once you have reaped enough information for one option, step back over the line to your starting position. If you are sitting, put the piece of paper down. Close your eyes, and place your hand on your heart if that helps. Take a deep breath, letting go of the previous option and clearing the way for the next. Don't miss this step.

5. Now choose another option and repeat the process above. Notice the differences in how each option feels.

By the end of this exercise, you will have a lot of useful data, which could be a mixture of any of the following:

Full yes, which you'll feel open and excited about, aligned with head, heart and gut.

Not quite a full yes, but there might be some appealing aspects, which you could consider. You might not want to live on an ashram, but perhaps something about travel, a more spiritual life or more structure appeals.

Full no.

Not quite a full no, but maybe not a priority for instance. You have to accept you can't do everything.

Here's what my client Jan came up with when we did this together:

Take a year out. She noticed her body relax. There were important things that she would have time to do, such as clear the house and spend more time with her children. Despite it not being financially viable at the moment, she could consider a shorter sabbatical later, her head suggested.

Apply for other jobs. She felt a strong 'no' in head, heart and gut. She hated the process of applying for jobs and sensed very clearly that a meaningful life for her wasn't going to be found in another similar role that would potentially present the same issues.

Volunteer. Although her head said yes, her heart felt very flat. It felt like something she wasn't ready for yet.

Dancer. She felt really energized. I asked her what appealed about it. 'Movement, connecting with people (she spent a lot of her time behind her desk), and also being creative.' This was vital, no matter what she did. Sometimes it's not the job description but something else about it that appeals.

Do more art. She noticed a tickle in her belly. It felt scary, yet exciting.

Join an ashram. She loved this idea, although she didn't want to do it. It appealed to her eccentric, curious side that enjoyed the unexpected, expanding her horizons and experiencing new things – part of herself that she had boxed away to do her job. No wonder she was discontented. However she was going to create a more meaningful life, it was going to include honouring this side of herself. What a lovely discovery.

Within a few weeks, Jan renegotiated with her employer to reduce her working days and change her manager, because the one she had at the time wasn't aligned with her values. She enrolled on an art course, and prepared herself to go freelance and move to another country as a future step. She'll tell you she's taken back her power, rather than feeling stuck and helpless.

Here's another option from one of my clients.

'Rajasthan.'

It was our last coaching session before Christmas, and as we sat in a hotel lobby with a pot of tea and plate of mince pies, Graham's eyes were glowing. One of the options he had come up with was a trip to northern India. Although it might not be possible immediately, something here was bringing him alive.

'What is it about Rajasthan?' I asked.

'I see streets full of colour and warmth. I hear beautiful music. I feel free.'

'And what would you like to take about this that you could have more of in your life now, even if you can't travel there at the moment?'

'Giving myself permission to feel free.'

Rajasthan. It's a state of being for Graham as much as a place. I imagine you now, with your own personal Rajasthan image alive somewhere in you. However it appears, don't box it away. Graham's first small step was to reorganize the leadership of his company so he was less involved in day-to-day operations. What neither of us knew then was that within a year his whole industry would receive a massive shock when the global Covid-19 pandemic hit. It was going to take longer, but even in the smallest moments of quiet in the storm, he could still visualize Rajasthan and the freedom he gave himself permission to dream about.

*

By now hopefully you have at least one option or elements to explore. These are your seeds. What do you do with them? In the next chapter, I am going to show you how to make a start by nurturing what you have separated out from the chaff with a four-stage process to Purpose, Nourish, Strengthen and Action. Onwards!

10. Nurture Your Ideas and Put Them into Action

Raise your hand if you've ever had an attack of the 'yes, buts'. You're in good company, so don't be ashamed. I certainly have them on a regular basis, and so do every one of my clients. If they show up during and after the decision-making game of the previous chapter, they are bang on time. They tend to pop up when you've come up with an option that could be the seed of a more meaningful life. There you are, all excited by a new possibility – it could be in your career, a project, a relationship, spiritual or emotional growth, or anything else – and boom – 'Yes, but . . . '. Just like that, they'll rip your idea to shreds with reasons why you shouldn't do it. You don't want to ignore them and sally forth blindly, but it helps to know the difference between realism and pessimism, truth and fear, and how to put this to work usefully. And help is at hand. You're going to take a seed idea from the previous chapter and nurture it enough that it can withstand the 'yes, buts', so that – even if you decide not to plant it – it's not the critic or saboteur making the decision for you. Then you are going to plan how to put that idea into action by doing small experiments, gathering important feedback from what you discover, and deciding on your next steps. Remember, life isn't an exam with a pass or fail grade. Trying will get you further than not trying.

How to Purpose, Nourish, Strengthen and Action Your Ideas

Think of yourself as the gardener of your life. You plant seeds in good soil and give them light, space, protection and nourishment – and sometimes prune, graft and replant. Knowing what is needed at each stage is essential to making anything grow and flourish.

However, our critics and saboteurs rush in to stamp on tender shoots. One of the ways you'll be able to spot their arrival is when you hear your inner talk say, 'Yes, but . . .' Every time I take a blank sheet of paper and a pencil, ready to plant my garden with a new creative project, my inner Auditor shows up with a hundred reasons why my delicate new idea could never be a revenue spinner. He's trying to keep me safe but – like all our 'shoulds', critics and saboteurs – he's a master at disguising himself as the voice of reality when actually he's juiced up on fear. There is a place for his measured pruning – just not at the beginning of the process.

Each stage of moving from ideas to action asks different types of attention from us in order. Where do you start? I coach leaders and notice how they can leap very quickly to coming up with a vision and a strategy, when it's important to align new ideas first with Purpose – their *why*. The process I suggest to them – and you – is purpose–vision–strategy: why, what and how. Once you know your seed ideas align with your *Purpose* and values, then you creatively explore and play with *what* your idea could be to *Nourish* your vision before you *Strengthen* your idea by thinking about your strategy – *how* you could make it real. As quickly as possible after that, you roll up your sleeves and get into *Action* to put energy out into the world with small, low-risk experiments and receive feedback, correcting course if necessary as you go along. Critics love to squash creativity, so the process coming up draws boundaries around each stage, so that ideas get to breathe before being audited.

Here's what you'll need to get started.

Space

- As with the decision-making game, it can help to physically move as this shifts your energy, which can stagnate when we sit at the same desk staring at screens all day. You can allocate different spaces in your home or around a table for each stage of the process and move to each in turn if it's possible for you.
- Sometimes getting out of your usual environment helps. You'll focus better when you're not in the same place as your laundry, washing-up or other distractions. Maybe there's a café, park, gallery, museum or library you could go to.

Time

- Some clients have taken half a day out to do this, and spent an hour on each stage. If that's not an option, then don't worry. I know it's not possible to stop the world. You can spend as little as fifteen minutes on each, which means you can do the whole process in an hour, with short breaks in between. It's a great exercise to do during a commute or when travelling.

- You don't have to do each stage in one sitting. You can allocate a day or week to each stage, and then spend between fifteen minutes and an hour on it at different times during that period.
- Take a break between each space to clear your head – even five minutes will help.

Focus

- Needless to say, you will need to minimize distractions. No phones, and, if you do this on a computer, turn your wi-fi off so you don't get alerts.
- Setting a timer can help. Promise yourself that whatever time you allocate, you're not going to do anything else but this. Make your coffee, finish your errands, ask your partner to not interrupt, see if someone can keep an eye on the kids, or take time when they are not around. Studies show that twenty-five minutes of focused attention gets you further than hours of multi-tasking.
- Use the mindfulness and centering practices from Chapter Two if you start to feel the itch to do something else. The best writing advice I ever received is genius: Sit. Stay.

Exercise:
Purpose–Nourish–Strengthen–Action

Stage One: Purpose

Take one option you would like to try from the previous chapter's decision-making game. Don't try to do more than one at any time. In Purposing, you connect to the big picture of *why* this could be a meaningful choice with these questions:

- Does this idea align with my values? Check your compass.
- Why am I the right person to do this? Why is it good that I do?
- How would it feel meaningful to me?
- How would it be a vehicle for my purpose?
- Will I regret not doing it?

Stage Two: Nourish

Now take this idea and playfully and creatively explore *what* it could be.

Rules for Nourishing:

- No critics, saboteurs or 'shoulds' allowed for a fixed period. Give yourself permission to nourish your idea without them. I thank my inner Auditor for trying to help and ask him to come back later in the process.

- The word 'but' is forbidden, as in, 'Yes, but . . .'
  Catch them and mindfully switch to 'Yes,
  and . . .' Build, don't block.
- Similarly, keep an eye out for 'should'. It might
  be coming from a script that's not authentically
  your own. See if you can exchange it for 'I
  want'.

Feed your idea with the following powerful questions:

- What part of this idea do I like best? What
  excites me about it?
- What if I took this part and scaled it up? If this
  idea is a four on the scale, what would a ten be?
- What might be the biggest possible benefit of
  this idea, for myself and others?

Stage Three: Strengthen

Once you have purposed and nourished an idea, then and
only then do you move on to Strengthening it. Don't
jump here too early – you need to give the idea some
muscle and backbone so it's more resilient. Otherwise it's
like asking a ninety-pound newbie to bench-press their
own weight on day one of training. You can always go
back and nourish your idea for a while if you need to, and
you'll have the opportunity to double-check Purpose
later. Powerful Strengthening questions focus on *how* to
do it. Don't confuse realism with pessimism. Hold back
from finding ways it *could not* be achieved and instead
focus on how it *could* be done.

- What resources do I need? What do I have to hand, and what do I need to obtain? How would I do that? Don't assume, check. Resources can include the following, and please add your own.
  - Information and knowledge
  - Education, training and skills
  - Space
  - Time
  - Energy
  - Technology
  - Services
  - Finance
  - Infrastructure and transport
  - People and community
- What preparation do I need to do?
- What's the time commitment per week? What can I reasonably give?
- What would an action plan look like, step by step?
- What is the timeline to realize it?
- What are the benefits, costs and risks if I do this – and if I don't?
- What sacrifices will I need to make? Am I prepared to make them?
- What am I ignoring? What are my blind spots? What will I do to reduce risk? (If you are not sure, ask a friend, but be discerning: with the best of intentions, some want to please you, others will tell you what would work for themselves.)

- What small, low-risk experiment could I do to dip my toe into the water?
- How would I measure progress and success, and review — not just what's happening but how I feel?

Check in again with some Purpose questions too, to see if your idea could be a meaningful one for you now you have an idea of how you could do it.

- How do I really feel about the idea now? Check in with head, heart and gut using the technique from the previous chapter. Feeling daunted is normal. If there's a full no or not quite a full yes, get curious and explore where that's coming from. Maybe there's another way to do this. Or maybe there's one part of it that appeals, which you could explore further.
- Does this idea still align with my values — not just in what it is but *how* I could do it, and who I would need to be to do it?
- If I do this, what will a day, a week or a year living this choice look like? How will my life look in a year's time, five years and ten years? Will I still be aligned with my values and purpose?

By Strengthening, you work your idea into something practical. It may be that you discover that you might not be able to do exactly what you want how and when you want. For instance, Maria realized that she needed to stay in her academic job for financial reasons, so she found therapy training that she could do part-time. It took her longer, but she got there. Don't stop at a block, keep focusing on how it could be done. Now you are ready to take action.

Stage Four: Action

Perfectionism is not your friend. Once you have a well-thought-through idea and plans for taking action, don't get stuck in analysis-paralysis, endlessly weighing up pros and cons, or finessing every tiny detail – start taking steps. More people fail by never trying. What small, low-risk experiment could you do to dip your toe into the water and test your idea? You don't have to make an immediate dramatic change. You could shadow someone, volunteer or take a class to find out more and discover how you feel.

If your mind has gone blank when you think of first steps you might take, here's a method I find useful. I was introduced to the Four Elements method by my teacher Mark Walsh to generate different ways to move forward. I like to take a piece of paper, divide it into four quadrants, write one element in each quadrant and come up with at least two things I could do in each.

- *Fire.* Be decisive, action and goal-focused. What do you say yes or no to? Decide on something to start the ball rolling this week and do it. No more talk or waiting – take action!
- *Water.* Who could you talk or connect with?

- *Earth.* Create a plan, check the details; what can you do to get organized?
- *Air.* What would inspire you, what would be the blue-sky-thinking, out-of-the-box creative thing to do?

If you don't have a clear idea of what you want to try, take a look at the Set Value-based Goals exercise from Chapter Four, in which you thought about ways you could honour your values and commit to action. You started by putting a value first and then crafting an action from there. Is there something there that you could take through the Purpose–Nourish–Strengthen–Action process to see if it could be worked up? Remember, this is not only about changing career, working for yourself or going back into education. It could just as well be a new location, better work–life balance, or prioritizing relationships, family, health, spirituality or creativity, for instance.

Here's how I have used this process in my own life. A while ago, I was lost. I had been made redundant from my previous job, although my ex-employer offered me some freelance facilitation work. I considered my options through the decision game, such as taking the freelance work, starting a business, looking for another salaried job in the same or another field, going back to a previous area of employment, taking time off, retraining, or joining that ashram. The facilitation work had my heart beating faster as I love supporting people who want to grow and wanted to be useful to them. I had also loved teaching in my previous academic career. But the Auditor arrived on cue – how was I ever going to support myself over the long term with intermittent fees? While this was important to consider, it was not a block to doing it; I just had to take it into account and figure out a way I could.

First, I checked my compass and considered the big picture in the Purpose stage.

- *Does this idea align with my values?*
  - Love & Connection – big yes: I will be working directly with people.
  - Growth & Learning and Exploration – another big yes: I will grow, learn and help others do the same.
  - Service – big yes again: I find a real sense of purpose in supporting people.
  - Creativity – absolutely: I won't thrive without it.
- *Why am I the right person to do this? Why is it good that I do?*
  - I care about people. I am good at and enjoy connecting with them. I know how to create powerful self-development workshops, have good presenting skills and relevant experience. I believe in this work because I know how it has helped me and others.
- *How would it feel meaningful to me?*
  - I could look back on my life and know that I helped people, and used my experience, values and skills to do that. I'd love to be able to say that I kept learning and growing as I did.

- *How would it be a vehicle for my purpose?*
  - I want to connect people – and myself – with our deeper potential. This would be why I would do this, and this is the person I want to be.
- *Will I regret not doing it?*
  - The opportunity is here now. Life is a gift. I'll never know what might happen unless I try.

I played with this seed idea and here's what I discovered in the Nourishing stage.

- *What part of this idea do I like best? What excites me most?*
  - Using my strengths, skills and experience to help others. Having direct connection with people. Being creative. Being my own boss and having a sustainable career.
- *What if I took this part and scaled it up? If this idea is a four on the scale, what would a ten be?*
  - Helping others through connecting with them is the best part. I could become a more skilful and effective facilitator by training as a coach, which would also give me another income stream, so I don't put all my eggs into one basket. Lightbulb moment! And a ten would be writing books as well as running my own workshops, courses and retreats.
- *What might be the biggest possible benefit of this idea, for myself and others?*
  - Helping people who will then support more people. Making a contribution to a world in

which people live more meaningful lives. Living a more authentic and meaningful life myself, feeling that in some small way I'm making a difference.

I had Purposed and Nourished my idea, now I needed to Strengthen it.

- *What resources do I need? What do I have to hand, and what do I need to obtain? How would I do that?*
  - To train as a coach I need to research the best courses, and have time and money to do it. To coach, I'll need to meet people at a location, to book one for workshops, or to use video platforms on my computer – and I'll need to learn how to do that. I'll also need to understand how to do my own taxes and I'll need insurance, accreditation, a website and marketing.
- *What help would I need to call in?*
  - I know some coaches and could find more on the internet. What would they recommend?
- *What preparation do I need to do?*
  - Build up my savings. Have a clear idea of what I need to live on. Figure out how to find clients, and how many I would need and what to charge so I could make a living. Create a website. Figure out what I need to do to be self-employed, for instance, get an accountant and take into account my future pension needs.

- *What is the timeline to realize it? What's the time commitment per week?*
  - I have enough money for a year if I top up with part-time work. Training is five months, during which I can create a website, and then give myself another six months to get enough clients to sustain myself. This leaves me with enough time to take up freelance work.
- *What would a rough action plan look like, step by step?*
  - December: Research training courses.
  - January: Take facilitation work.
  - February: Start training.
  - April: Aim to have website built and email set up. Get insurance.
  - June: Complete training.
  - June to December: Recruit clients, review income and outgoings monthly, and adjust if necessary. Review at end of year to see if current plan is sustainable.
- *What are the benefits, costs and risks if I do this – and if I don't?*
  - *Benefit of doing:* I would be autonomous and fulfilled, I can coach until I retire – and beyond. Living my values and a more meaningful life.
  - *Benefit of not doing:* Security, ability to get a mortgage in the short term.
  - *Costs of doing:* Nearly a year living off savings and short-term contract work, continuing to rent for a few years until I can qualify again for a mortgage.

- *Costs of not doing:* Working for someone else. Risks of future redundancy. Not fulfilling my potential. Future regret.
- *What sacrifices will I need to make? Am I prepared to make them?*
  - Loss of savings and income in the short term. Time spent pitching for work. I am prepared to make them for a year.
- *What am I ignoring? What are my blind spots? What will I do to reduce risk?*
  - Check business costs of coaching and consider what happens if I don't get clients. Reduce overheads until my business ramps up. Add a cut-off date by which if I am not earning a living, I explore other options. Being a trained coach and experienced facilitator could be a great addition to my CV if I have to go back into the job market. Economic downturns and sickness could affect my income, and I need to diversify my revenue streams, investigate insurance and keep a minimum savings level to sustain me for 3–6 months.
- *What small, low-risk experiment could I do to dip my toe into the water?*
  - Some coach-training programmes offer an introductory taster weekend, so I could understand more about coaching and have the opportunity to practise it.
- *How would I measure progress and success, and review?*
  - Review finances and client base every month. Keep checking in with my values compass, and with my head, heart and gut.

I checked my idea with some Purpose questions.

- *How do I really feel about the idea now I have looked at what it could be and how I could do it?*
  - My head says I can trial it safely.
  - My heart says I long to be doing this work.
  - My gut says I have been given this opportunity; I don't want to miss it by saying no. I trust I have everything I need and can learn.
- *Does this idea still align with my values – not just in what it is but how I could do it, and who I would need to be to do it?*
  - Yes, I still believe it is. I will need to remind myself to keep checking in as I go along, and remember why I am doing it, so I don't get lost.
- *If I do this, what will a day, a week or a year living this choice look like? How will my life look in a year's time, five years and ten years? Will I still be aligned with my values and purpose?*
  - Day – Meeting clients during day. Will be tiring, so I need to commit to rest and self-care.
  - Week – balance of creativity, writing and facilitation, creating pitches and programmes, marketing, coaching. I like variety.
  - Year – possible downturn in coaching and facilitating during summer and Christmas holidays.
  - One year's time – building a sustainable business.

- Five years – achieving stability.
- Ten years – having a business that grows and flexes to changes in my life.
- I feel I can do this and be in alignment with my values of Love & Connection, Growth and Service, and I will do a check every month to make sure and adjust if not.

Then I created first-step actions that I could start doing that week. It's important to get into action as soon as possible, so you can start to build momentum. Change happens in small steps that lead to bigger ones. You'll start to feel positive too and that will give you energy and the ability to see more opportunities as you move.

- *Fire.*
  - Make a decision to take the facilitation work.
- *Water.*
  - Arrange to talk with coach friends.
- *Earth.*
  - Create a spreadsheet with a financial plan. Research and compare coach training, accreditation and insurance.
- *Air.*
  - Set aside time to think creatively about who I would appeal to as a coach; what's my pitch? What workshops would I like to create and where could I lead them?

This process gave me something clear and solid to aim for, rather than trying to avoid short-term uncertainty and anxiety. I had a plan. Although there were some unknowns ahead and it felt a bit overwhelming, I took good lessons from my love of walking – charting a course, packing my bag with what I needed, lacing up my walking boots and taking the first step (my Mountaineer ally from Chapter Eight was a great companion). I was creating a new authentic life for myself, rather than reacting to fear (self-employment is uncertain), to old scripts (I have to have a salaried job) or internalizing life events (I have been made redundant again; I must be useless).

Seeing yourself as the gardener – the creator or artist of your life – is empowering and liberating. You last met Ali in Chapter Six. She has been through many acts in her life and is working on her next chapter. She inspired me as she told me:

'We are our own greatest works of art. There isn't a standard that we have to adhere to. Our job is to be ourselves and evolve and develop, and that feels to me to be incredibly liberating.'

Small Steps and Experiments

My interviewee Bruce said something very wise to keep in mind,

'You'll always keep learning, it's never finished. I think this is the point, really, isn't it? Always keep learning. Always keep using your experiences to inform you about the next step and the next step.'

Small actions send a message simultaneously to our deeper selves and into the wider world, where it attracts energy, as games-developer Adam discovered when – as an experiment – he wrote a blog post about his idea that games could cultivate nature connection to see what response it received.

'It had lots of baffled reactions. But one guy sees it and gets in touch. He runs the climate regeneration fund at a big firm. He is just a regular-looking dude in a Patagonia fleece. I was expecting him to go, "I've worked at this company, and I've done all of these things." Instead, he tells me his story of having an undiagnosed illness that lasted for about eight years of his life, and how that shifted him to finding meaning. And he read my post about my struggles and what gave my life meaning now and he called me.'

Sometimes a small act is all you can do, for many reasons, but don't be put off by the idea that you need to change your life with a big, bold action overnight. Change actually happens in a thousand small steps. Ali calls these small shifts 'tectonic interventions', which shift the bedrock of habitual life to let more air and light in. After a serious bout of Covid, she decided to try her own small experiments, focusing on what she was reasonably able to do at the time without risk.

'The first week I had Covid, I couldn't get out of bed. Then I could walk ten yards, then maybe it's twenty-five yards. I called it my convalescence project – only doing stuff that fulfils me, makes me feel well, gives me what I need. As I was walking, I would really notice the plants around me. I'd already started painting, but my energy wouldn't give me what I needed to paint in the way that I wanted to.

'And when my energy was right, I'd make them into a monoprint. Capturing the life of the plant seemed to, in turn, feed my own energy source. For me, my art is calling and it's time for it to be given space to express itself and that's a wonderful thing.'

She recently exhibited her work at a gallery. The small tectonic interventions led her there, with each small choice leading to the next.

Gather Data

When you are finding your own path, small, low-risk experiments allow you to gather data. You can always change tack and adapt based on what you discover through regular self-reflection check-ins to ask yourself.

Journal Questions

- What is the experience like? What am I feeling? (Your feelings are vital data.)
- What am I learning?
- How would I apply what I am feeling and learning?
- Based on the above, what's my next small step?

It may be that what looked promising at the beginning runs into a dead end. You might have thought living in the country would be a great idea, so you did a small experiment and rented a place for a month, only to find that you needed a car for everything and felt isolated. That's useful data. Knowing that, what's your next step? It's an illusion to believe that your path lies all ready-made before you, like the yellow brick road in *The Wizard of Oz*. You're creating it yourself as you go along. Failure is part of the process – you just found out a way it won't work or a route you don't want to take. I discovered coaching more than four clients a day exhausted me, and wasn't great for my fifth client of the day either. It didn't mean I quit coaching, I just knew I had to draw boundaries and not rely on coaching for my sole income. Trying and learning isn't only the way to find your path, it *is* your path.

Don't forget, change is a process of *transition*, and it's not always all or nothing. Bruce didn't give up the accounting day job that gave him security. He also trained as a coach and then went to four days accounting, one coaching, and then shifted again when he felt ready. It took a few years to find a balance that met all his needs:

'It gives me breathing space. I don't have the pressure of worrying about finding ten clients to pay my bills.'

After realizing the juice wasn't worth the squeeze in his sales job – even though it allowed him to own a big house and expensive car – Eric also retrained, and kept his options open for consultancy work in his old field, which to this day provides him with a solid baseline to do other things and offers a fallback should he need it. Jan reduced her working hours and used some of the time to enrol on an art course and to plan a future move. Devon took a job that helped him pay off his debts, so that when he was ready, he could experiment and dip his toe back into performing. Maria did some courses to see if being a therapist might work for her, and then kept teaching whilst she retrained part-time. Yasmin worked in a café and a food project for a while, so she could learn about making food in order to write food books well. Dalia needed to set boundaries, so she had time and energy to network and plan her exit from the corporate job that was making her unhappy. Eva ran a few standalone workshops for young women before she felt experienced and informed enough to give up her day job and invest in building a platform. It took Charley six years after she left the military to find a life she didn't need a holiday from, and she tried a few avenues before she realized that what lit her up was helping others, and then she had to figure out how to make a living from that. Adam had to tend to his well-being, physically, mentally and spiritually, before he could create and pitch new ideas – and what he discovered in the first phase informed the second greatly. Rachel kept working and looking for other opportunities on one hand, whilst improving her finances and building up her savings so she would have security. Pratam mentored, before setting up a mentoring programme for young men of colour like himself. Alana still had to figure out her energy levels by trial and error, continually clarifying what's really important for her. Graham trialled spending more time in the country, handing over operations and doing more creative projects, until he could make a more permanent move. Rajasthan would have to wait, but Norfolk was where he could find that freedom in small doses at first. All of them experienced dead ends and unexpected setbacks. As I mentioned at the beginning of the book, life isn't a straight line. In the next chapter, I'll offer ways to help recover and grow from those challenges.

Work to Make Your Decision the Right One

Finally, remember that there is no 'perfect' decision. There are a few misconceptions about life decisions. Sometimes we can have a vision, set a goal and imagine that once we have arrived at the promised land, then the work stops. It doesn't.

In the American National Football League, the person awarded Most Valuable Player the most times to date is Peyton Manning. At a certain point in his career, he found himself out of contract, meaning he was a free agent and could join any team he wanted. Needless to say, he was courted by several of the major teams. He took his time making a choice. This would be the place where he would end his career, and he wanted a location his family liked, with good schools and churches, so this was an important life decision. For months, the media followed his every move, hoping to get the scoop on his choice. Finally, he announced he was joining the Denver Broncos, and when journalists pressed him to reveal why there above all other options, he replied that they all were pretty great, which had made it difficult to choose. Until he had had an important insight: there wasn't a choice that was more 'right' than any other; he had to make a decision, and then work to make it the right one.

I want you to read that last sentence again.

The answer is not out there for you to find. The ability to build a meaningful life is within you, and is created and sustained depending on the work you are committing to do to make it the right one. We imagine that if we spend hours in research and development, diving into the web, scouting locations and talking with people, we'll alight on that one essential piece of data that will make the choice clear. But the most important data is how you feel, and the most important stance is the commitment you bring.

You're on your way. In the next chapter, I am going to encourage you to practise consistency and patience, and build resilience. This is not a detour from our path to a more meaningful life. A meaningful life is not one in which you are happy all the time. It has challenges, and it's how we face them that makes life meaningful.

11. Raise Your Resilience

Let me lie to you. Finding your own path is easy. With this book, you receive a magic pill that will make everything simple and straightforward. You'll be able to live how you want, where you want, with whom you want, without difficulty or setbacks. You'll have perfect health all your life. Everything you do will be successful. No one you love will suffer. Life will be fair. To be honest, I'd like that pill too. That is, until I consider that all my struggles have made me who I am. If I hadn't had to persevere and dig myself out of holes, I wouldn't know I could. I wouldn't even know how to use a spade. You are doing the messy, brave work of finding your own path. I salute you, but it would be dishonest not to let you know that building and living a meaningful life is not without challenges, hard work, setbacks and difficulties. Some come from within, and some from without. Life is harder for some than for others. The idea that you can pull yourself up by the bootlaces only applies if you have them or if they aren't continually snipped away. What seems like good fortune can be privilege. We live within systems that do not offer level playing fields for everyone, and sometimes life will throw curveballs that change things forever. All I can do here is offer some help with developing resilience, because I hope you keep going. The fact that your path doesn't instantly appear and challenges do doesn't mean you are failing or that you have made a huge mistake. Learning ways to keep going and grow from the challenges *is* your path; more than this, it defines it. Your response to difficulties holds the medicine you need to create your future.

Imagine you are walking the path of a more meaningful life and you trip on a pothole. You can curse yourself for not seeing it, curse your footwear, curse the local council for not filling it in or curse the path for being treacherous. Or you can say, as much as is within my power, what do I need to have a firmer grip on the path and recover from any mishaps, because it will be rough in places? Remember what you have already gleaned from this book. You know how to find time and space for yourself to reflect. You can bring your attention to the here and now and lower your stress with mindfulness and centering practices. You have a compass aligned to your North Star, and your values and sense of purpose are there to guide you. You know how to manage your energy. You can reduce the power of inner critics and saboteurs, and connect with inner and outer allies to support you. You have tools to generate options, make decisions and bring nascent ideas into action. Stress makes you feel small, alone, and narrows your perspective. We have a tendency to over-identify with setbacks. As my wise inner ally reminded me, this book might not be perfect, but that doesn't mean I am a failure as a human being. Remember, you are bigger than the setback and stress, and your path is more than the pothole.

Before introducing you to exercises and a framework that will help, I want to make one important thing clear.

Everybody has different resilience levels, so we do not start from the same place, and each of us will have different patterns and challenges when faced with adversity. Your resilience is affected by your birth mother's anxiety when you were in the womb, your parents' stress levels, your life experiences, especially in childhood, and by trauma – not only that caused by a one-off event but also ongoing stress, such as that caused by abuse, neglect, loss, conflict, war, bullying, systemic prejudice, social injustice, poverty, oppression, discrimination and victimization, and this can affect many generations down. If any of this applies to you, I am sorry. I do recommend you seek support, especially trauma-informed therapy, which includes working at the level of the body, and I give some suggestions at the end of this book. There is no shame if your resilience levels are affected. There is no way that anyone should be, no ideal, no stiff upper lip you have to adopt. What follows can help to raise your resilience level from wherever you are, hopefully towards more of what you need.

Know Your Resources

To start, remember your own stories. As you have already discovered, the stories you tell about yourself are full of your past resources, which you can mine for the present and future. In Chapter Three, you started the conversation with yourself, telling yourself the story of when you made a positive choice in your life, to see what was important about that. Now you're going to look at when things didn't go to plan to remind yourself how far you have already come, and what resources helped you.

Exercise: Your Resilience Story

However suits you, create a timeline of your life in your journal.

Include moments when something didn't go how you wished – perhaps a job that didn't work out, a project that failed, a relationship that ended, or somewhere you left. It might have been a personal crisis such as an illness, loss or redundancy, or a national or local one, such as a pandemic, political, economic or community change. If there is an event that is very traumatic and/or unresolved, and this brings up painful emotions, then please go easy. You might not want to revisit this today, and that's perfectly okay.

Note down the following:

- How you chose to respond. What did you choose to do and be? What was important to you about this?
- On a separate page, draw a line down the middle. In one column write down the *inner* resources you drew upon. Take your time with this and the external resources below, as sometimes you may have forgotten or not used them for a while.

Strengths: for instance, attention to detail, perseverance.
Values: knowing what's important for you, such as treating people well, being creative, finding

opportunity for growth, or seeing what would give you a sense of achievement.

Actions: for instance, exercise, giving yourself time and space to reflect and work on a plan, researching, seeking help, or practising gratitude.

- In the other column, write down *external* resources you drew upon.

  Connections: such as friends and teachers, or communities.

  Sources of information and support: such as advice centres, books, legal or medical experts, websites, social media accounts, podcasts, a favourite place in nature, poems, sayings or music. One of my clients has a saying she keeps posted above her desk – 'This too shall pass' – which helps her keep perspective when things get rough.

One more thing to do. Ask what would you like to give yourself credit for? Too often we forget what we have overcome, when we think about difficulties we have struggled through, overlooking our resourcefulness and resilience. From looking at my darkest times, I can give myself credit for self-compassion, digging deep and taking action in small steps.

Build your inner and outer resources in the good times, as they will be there for you when the going gets tough. Keep your list handy and add to it. Do something once a week to make an investment in them. If you notice your resource lists are lacking, then make a commitment to add more. Every one of my clients has spoken of the benefits of small regular investments in their resilience banks. From Mia, whose meditation practice helped stabilize her when she lost her income and home during Covid, to Devon, who built a strong community with people who were able and willing to help him when he struggled.

Grow from Challenge

The journey to create a more authentic, meaningful life hasn't been smooth for most of my clients. Yasmin agreed to talk with me for this book, partly because – although she is now a successful writer – it took patience and grit, and the capacity not to take a rejection or setback as the final word on her ability to create a new path for herself.

'It took time to write a book because it was a craft I had to learn. I'd never done it before. My first book proposal didn't get any interest from agents. It's really easy to take rejection as a sign. But it doesn't necessarily mean a project or something about you isn't right. I took it as a sign that I needed to improve and communicate it better. I wrote to other authors and asked them for advice. I did a fundraiser online. I decided I needed work experience in the field, so I managed a community kitchen and worked in a café. I had a master's degree and I was making coffees for minimum wage. I think it is this kind of commitment that you have to have. Success doesn't come without making some sacrifices, things being difficult, and sticking with it. I genuinely believe that if you do stick with something, work hard at it and take every bit of feedback as a message for how you could improve, as opposed to being wounded by it, that's going to make all the difference. I went back to literary agents with a year's worth of experience and sample material in a book proposal and there was a bidding war. Seven years later – three best-selling books, all critically acclaimed. If I'd said at that moment when those agents rejected me, "This isn't going to work," I wouldn't be where I am now.'

Yasmin still struggles at times. Being a writer – even one with best-selling books – is precarious financially, even as she acknowledges that owning a home is a privilege that not everyone shares. Agents and publishers can still reject her proposals, especially if they don't conform to a winning formula. Her challenges continue. Her point is that your response can affect the outcome.

When I work with clients who are struggling with adversity or a setback, I ask them to follow a sequence of three steps, which can help them recover and even grow.

1. Acknowledge Your Emotions

When adversity hits, we can skip over this and go into 'fixing' mode, but this is an essential first step. When we resist or avoid feeling what we are feeling, it leads to three problems.

One, unacknowledged emotions don't go away, they tend to leak back indirectly, showing up as overreactions to small events, stress, pain and sickness, anxiety and depression.

Two, when we avoid our difficult emotions, or bypass them with false positivity – looking for the silver lining in everything, even the most painful experiences – we lower our resilience. And if we habitually numb them, for instance with alcohol or drugs, they don't go away, and numbing strategies can cause more problems.

Finally, we can't take action to alleviate it. Sometimes we shield feeling vulnerable with other emotions to try and protect ourselves from discomfort. I remember a time when I was lonely after a break-up. I felt *angry* because I felt it was unjust that I was lonely. I also felt *ashamed* of feeling lonely, as if I was fundamentally unlovable (old core beliefs rise like zombies when things don't go our way). Then I decided to surrender and allow myself to feel what was going on underneath. Rather than saying, 'I *am* lonely' and over-identifying with a state, I said, 'I *feel* lonely.' It helps to be able to name how you feel with more accuracy. There is a difference between stress and disappointment, anger and fear, hurt and worry, depression and loneliness. I recommend looking up the wheel of emotions online to expand your emotional vocabulary. Our emotions need our acknowledgement first, and then we can take action to help.

Remember Dalia, whom you met in Chapter Eight? Because she wasn't acknowledging how angry and hurt she felt by her boss's behaviour, she couldn't give herself compassion, identify that her boundaries were being crossed, and so do something about it. Devon felt ashamed at not having money, and judged himself harshly. When he finally acknowledged that he felt vulnerable, and that that was understandable, he could take better care of himself, start to separate his self-worth from his financial worth, and act to change his circumstances.

The Five As practice from Chapter Eight can be very helpful in allowing the part of you that is feeling the strong emotion to speak directly. Here's another of the simplest and most effective techniques I know for accepting and acknowledging rough emotions.

Practice: The Breath of Kindness

- Softly breathe in to the count of four (deep breathing can trigger a panic response when you are in crisis, so please start gently) and as you do, imagine that your breath connects with all the feelings inside you at this moment, including hurt, anger, loss and disappointment.
- Gently breathe out to the count of four. As you exhale, offer all those feelings acceptance, kindness and compassion.

This practice is not about trying to change how you feel but helping you accept it without clinging to it. It helps to remember that we are people having emotions, they don't have us. One of my Buddhist teachers asked me to imagine emotions as clouds. They pass, but the sky remains the same. This isn't to diminish our emotions, or avoid them, but to believe they are normal, understandable, impermanent, and we can survive them.

Sometimes emotions don't move for a while. If you find

yourself chronically stuck with difficult emotions, then please seek professional help from a medical professional or therapist. I have added resources at the end of this book.

2. Self-care

We can have some unhelpful ideas of what self-care looks like. When you experience setbacks or difficulties and have a perfectly understandable strong emotion, getting drunk, scrolling social media or lighting a scented candle is not going to address your suffering. Without proper self-care (see the list below), you won't be reaching the parts that need attention.

I know for myself that when a crisis hits, I have about thirty-six hours of fully triggered anxiety – the kind that's about an eight or nine on the scale. My mind floods with images of catastrophes so vivid I believe they are going to come true. I react as much to those fevered imaginings as to the event itself. It's as if I am living a movie, one in which the story stops at a disaster: the Nazis seize the Ark of the Covenant and Indiana Jones is shut into the Well of Souls with thousands of snakes; T'Challa has just been defeated in ritual combat and has fallen into the ravine; and Ripley is abandoned on an exploding platform, facing the alien queen with no more ammunition. But in our moment of crisis, we can forget that the story keeps going, and that we can get in the director's chair and have a say in what happens next. To do this, it helps to get ourselves into as good a state as possible.

Being aware of my tendencies and patterns when

adversity hits, I know I need to self-care as much as possible in those first thirty-six hours, with some of the practices I have listed below. You can build your own self-awareness by reflecting on these questions in your journal:

Journal Questions

- When challenge hits, what's my typical reaction?
- How long does that first stress reaction typically last?
- What can I do to take care of myself? What helps? What doesn't?
- Knowing that I have overcome many challenges in my life already, what can I say to myself to remind me of this when another one arrives? The resources you identified from the Your Resilience Story exercise will be a treasure chest.

Have an emotional first-aid kit of practices and tools to help you self-care in difficult times. Take a look at Chapter Six and pay special attention to replenishing your emotional, physical and spiritual energy, which can be very affected by adversity. Here are some of the other exercises and practices from this book that you can put in your kit.

- Revisiting and rewriting operating fictions (Chapter One)
- Here I Am mindfulness practice (Chapter Two)

- Centering and Six Directions Breathing (Chapter Two)
- Self-reflection Questions (Chapter Three)
- 'Hello, Goodbye' Practice for Letting Go (Chapter Five)
- Writing back to critics and saboteurs (Chapter Seven)
- Self-compassion practice (Chapter Seven)
- Soothing Your Inner Child with the Five As (Chapter Eight)
- Cultivating inner allies (Chapter Eight)

What else helps relieve stress and anxiety?

- Talking with a friend, counsellor or therapist.
- Breathing techniques, such as lengthening your out-breath to switch on your parasympathetic nervous system, which acts like a sprinkler in a fire. Techniques such as counting 4-6-8 – counting four on an inhale, holding for six, and exhaling for eight – help you do this.
- Time in nature.
- Yoga, meditation and mindfulness.
- Exercise.
- Sleep and rest.
- Healthy diet.
- Journalling.
- Cognitive behavioural therapy (CBT).

Once you have taken the first two steps, you are ready for the third.

3. See Where You Are Now as a Threshold

Reframe this moment as a threshold, a fork in the road where you have choice over what to do and be next. After Dalia and Devon had acknowledged how they felt and taken care of themselves, they felt ready to make some decisions, which for both of them meant creating a plan B, rather than expecting the situations they were in would magically go away. You may not have chosen the situation in which you find yourself, but you *are* choosing how to respond. Stress makes us forget that we have this choice. Here's an exercise that can help.

Exercise: Create the Story You Want to Live

1. Divide a page in your journal into seven columns.
2. Write headings for each column in this order:
   - The Event (what has happened or is happening)
   - Tomorrow
   - One week
   - One month
   - Three months
   - Six months
   - One year
3. In the first column, succinctly describe the situation you are in.
4. In each of the following columns, under the headings above, write down:

- actions you intend to take (you may only be able to do this for the first few); and
- how you want to feel.

This allows you to start feeling some agency over what happens next. Sometimes it's difficult to see a year ahead clearly, especially in terms of actions, but envisaging how you want to feel is vital. The movie will keep running – as far as possible, be in the director's chair for the next part.

At this threshold, remind yourself of your values – what's important to you – and the big picture of how you want to live your life. You can revisit the exercises and practices in this book, especially in Chapters Four and Five, to help. I value Love, Growth, Service and Creativity. In times of trouble, I reach for these and recommit to them. My inner ally is particularly good at articulating them to me, when I have forgotten them. They are your guiding light and will help you see the path ahead. When you articulate them, you shift perspective to what's important about the decisions you want to make and the life you want to live from now on.

Journal Questions

When you face a challenge, ask yourself:

- How does this situation help me to see what's truly important and precious about my life?
- What would I say to a friend who is going through a similar struggle?

- How do I want to live my life from now on, so that I bring in more of what's important and meaningful for me now?

I often wish that life was easier, and I am sure that you do too. Our human predicaments deserve our humility, acceptance and compassion. A wise friend of mine, in her eighties, told me that growing older isn't for cissies. Life will bring you challenges you may feel you can never control or overcome. Some you can't.

Another friend developed an aggressive form of cancer in her early forties. She did all she could on many levels – medically, spiritually and emotionally, through every glimmer of hope and every trough of disappointment. I was deeply moved by her resilience under such extreme circumstances. The last time I saw her, she told me that in spite of everything, she hadn't felt as much joy in her life since she was four years old, and this gave her a sense of meaning. The work she did to build her resilience gave her something she wouldn't have had otherwise, although neither she nor anyone else would have wished such a challenge upon her. At the end, when all possibility of cure was gone, she surrendered, and returned to her island home to die surrounded by those who loved her, and her ashes were given to the sea on the beach where that four-year-old girl had played.

When you are forging your own path, rather than following one laid out for you, it can take a while, and there may be setbacks. You cut your way through some undergrowth, only to find yourself on the edge of a great chasm or river you need to cross. Sometimes, you can't, and you need to find another way. As I mentioned in the introduction, the belief that you can simply dream it and be it is not very helpful at these times. We can start to feel like failures. There are some reframes here I want you to take on board:

- Just because something is difficult doesn't mean it's impossible.
- Sometimes your path is defined as much by the doors that close behind you as by the ones that open in front.
- Just because something takes time doesn't mean it's not happening. Some clients feel impatient or frustrated occasionally, believing that seeing dramatic outcomes immediately or consistently is essential. It helps to remind ourselves that everything has its seasons. During winter, it might seem that nothing is happening, but a tree isn't dead in winter. It will blossom in spring.
- Life isn't an exam with a pass or fail grade at the end.
- When you fail, you have only discovered one way something can't be done, which is a step closer to discovering how it can. I once saw a picture representing what hope looked like, which showed a picture of a mountain with many paths to the summit.
- The smallest changes bring huge effects, as do inner ones. For many clients, just working on their relationship with inner critics and saboteurs changes their lives radically.

- Ultimately, the meaning of your life isn't determined by your struggles and disappointments. It's to be found in how you face them.
- Finally, sometimes we need to discern what is in our power to change, and accept what we can't.

You started this chapter by telling your story. Everyone else has theirs too. It's very human to struggle at times. Nobody else has a magic pill either. Adversity can help us connect more kindly with others, and with our shared humanity. As you move to the final step on your ongoing path to a more meaningful life, you're taking the story of finding your path with you, not only to support yourself but others too.

12. Tell Your Story

By the ruins of the old chapel, under grey Irish skies, I sat on the grass next to my mother's grave, and the words came simply: 'Hello, I found you again.' It wasn't just my mother I found, it was – in the most essential ways possible – myself. It's a story about changing my life from the inside out, and it isn't over yet. It's the story of how I connected more with my authentic self, so that I could bring more of myself into the world – both personally and professionally. It is the story of how I want to live my life now, and it's one which I write myself, rather than being dictated to me by internal and external 'shoulds', by my reactions and habits rather than conscious choices, or by the chorus of inner critics and saboteurs. I have more of a sense of who I am at heart, and see how my life might have a positive impact in the time I have. It's a more meaningful life than the one I had before, still with struggles and challenges, but now with more ways through them. It's the story that my clients and others are writing. It's the story I hope you can now begin to write and live for yourself.

When I trained as a life coach, I was told to resist sharing my own personal experience with clients. It's not about me, after all. When I came to write this book, the cursor winking at me intimidatingly from the top of a blank page, I knew I wanted to start with my story, although my heart trembled in my chest and my hands shook. My inner critics and saboteurs gathered around. 'You must be crazy. How narcissistic. Too exposing.' But what if it's not just about me? What if all our endeavours to find our own paths in life are not solely about us? What if they might be of service to others? I hoped that by telling you my story, you might feel a little less alone, a little less susceptible to the illusion that there's a party going on somewhere full of people who don't feel lost or struggle at times, and you're not on the list. If you are living your life right, it will bring challenge to your door, while struggle will be sitting on your sofa, asking what's for dinner. What if by writing and telling your story – of how you welcomed challenge in, and managed your struggles in a way that gave you a better relationship not only with them but with your resources and with yourself, you help others to write and live their own? What if this is one of the vital ways that – no matter what you do – your life is meaningful because of the positive impact you have on others?

This perspective can help on your journey. Many times, as a coach, I have sat with someone on the cusp of stepping across the threshold, sometimes even as they are about to place their foot on the new path of their lives. At a point such as this, you – like them and me – might hesitate and ask, 'Who am I, to do this?' The question that can get us unstuck is 'What if it's not just about you?'

Eva broke into a huge grin when I asked her this. She had had a moment of emotional vertigo – that experience when you stand at the edge between where you are now, with a step to take towards your path, and you suddenly feel dizzy and scared. When your life is expanding, it's natural to feel it at times. Eva was feeling overwhelmed because she was about to change her life: to leave behind how she had been living before – waiting for people to offer her work in a field she had fallen out of love with – and step across the threshold to create a community to support young entrepreneurs. She worried she wasn't good enough. But when I asked her to shift perspective to others, it released her fear, like someone suffering vertigo can sometimes shift it by looking to the horizon, rather than the drop. Every day now she wakes up and motivates herself by recalling that it's not just about her. So as the final step on this roadmap, I want you to tell your own story for yourself and for others.

Tell Your Story for You

The stories you tell yourself about yourself – whether explicit or implicit – have a significant effect on you. So much of what you do in your life is based on the story you tell yourself about who you think you were, are now and could be. When you step across the threshold to create a more meaningful life, you create new stories, each one a thread. Every time you do something that creates a change in how you feel, think and respond, you strengthen that thread with another, and then another, until it securely binds you to the life you can now lead – the life that may have once seemed impossible. As the storyteller of your life, you don't just organize and explain what happened in the past, you create expectations of what your future might look like which guide your actions in the present. Without giving yourself the power to do this by writing your own story, you stay trapped in the past, can't think new thoughts and make new choices.

Exercise: Be Your Own Storyteller

The first person who needs to hear your story is you. Take a look now at your story. It will help to set aside some time to read through your journal. Here are some of my favourite questions to help you reflect:

- If your life is a story, what is the title of the most recent chapter?
- What is its last sentence?
- If where you are now is at the start of a new chapter in your life story, what is the title?
- What is its first line?
- What is its last?
- What's the title of the next chapter?
- What is its first line?

What is the story you want to write? And what is the story you want to tell? There's something about understanding your life as a series of chapters, and as a whole story, that gives you permission to be its author.

When you look back on your life, you might feel that you have nothing to tell, that your life is unremarkable, but this isn't true. I have never failed to be blown away by the stories I hear. It's not just certain stories that are worth writing – of lofty historical figures, or of people who overcame extreme odds, and those who have found great fame, or infamy. Just as the old adage states that 'everyone is in a struggle you know nothing about', so I say 'everyone carries a story'. I recommend that you take some time around a birthday (especially the big ones) to write a mini biography. Trust me, you will have something to write. Sometimes I am asked who my heroes are, and my response is always the same: people. Whether friends, family or the people I meet and others I coach, when I hear the story of another human being – it's humbling and inspiring. Just living a human life with its struggles, challenges, gifts and loss makes you a hero in my book.

When I look at my life as a story from the past through the present to the future, I appreciate what I have learned along the way, and how that has made me who I am now. That gives me a sense of meaning – that my life is a journey, rather than a series of random events. Can you see the journey of your life? At times within this book, I have encouraged you to time-travel and reap resources from the past, present and future. One of the sweetest exercises I know for harnessing this is called Letters to Myself, so get ready to time-travel again.

Exercise: Letters to Myself

Part One: Past

Visualize yourself at a date from your past. It could be a year ago; it could be longer ago, perhaps when you were much younger.

Write your past self a letter:

- What do you want your past self to know?
- What can you tell your past self now that you wouldn't have been aware of then that might be helpful?
- What do you want to thank your past self for?

Part Two: Future

Visualize yourself at a date in the next five years.

Write your future self a letter from where you are today.

- What do you want your future self to know?
- What do you want to remind your future self you have in terms of inner and outer resources?

Take this letter and place it somewhere you'll be able to find it. Set a reminder in your diary for the date you chose, and when that day comes, find that letter again and read it.

Tell Your Story for Others

The second step is to tell your story to others. You don't have to hire an auditorium or start a YouTube channel. You don't have to write a book. You don't even have to speak. You tell your story in how you live your life. When you listen to someone or are kind, you tell your story of compassion and empathy. When you open your heart to laughter, play and love, when you respond rather than react to challenges, when you take the wheel of your life in your hands, you tell the story you have chosen to live.

The notion that you are separate from others is an illusion. You are part of a wider ecosystem, all connected, not only with people you know and meet but also with those with whom you may never have any direct dealings, even future generations. If people hadn't shared their own stories with me, I would never have realized that I too could choose to live a different life from the one I was then living. Although you might not realize it, your story is a torch that doesn't just light your way but can offer guidance, support, inspiration, acceptance and understanding to others. All of us struggle at times. What if what you have learned on your journey could offer help to someone who is finding life hard? What if you brought this more into your projects, families, communities, organizations and businesses? With massive rises in mental health issues and social division, and in a world that seems increasingly unstable and uncertain, we can all play a part in affecting wider systemic problems, no matter how small our contributions may seem. Let's not hoard what we have, or despair that we can't make a difference.

Before I finish, I want to give you an update on the stories of the people who have shared their stories with you in this book. It's hard to encapsulate each in one short paragraph, but here goes.

- Once an unhappily married salesperson who had become overweight, Eric is now fit and healthy physically, emotionally and spiritually. He leads several projects to improve trust between people, including in the workplace, where he can use his corporate knowledge and experience with his new skills. He has new, enriching relationships, and his children all say they have respect and admiration for his new path.

- Games developer and entrepreneur Adam needed to heal after his burnout, and what he discovered about himself and the benefits of nature and spirituality, he folds into his next projects. He now lives in the country with his family.
- Charley left her career in the military, retrained, met her husband and now lives abroad, helping people suffering with burnout. She lives a life from which she doesn't need to take a holiday.
- Yasmin has written several best-selling books and is getting ready for another big shift to write about culture and social justice.
- Graham is still running his company, now with a vision and plan for what a fulfilling phased retirement might look like. He is giving himself permission to spend more time in Norfolk, because this is what *he* needs.
- Rachel, the sales executive in her thirties, took more control of her finances, enabling her to explore other passions in her life.
- Maria left her husband and her academic job, made a permanent move to the country and qualified as a therapist. She opened her own

practice, offering a sliding scale of fees to serve her community.

- Ali now exhibits and sells her art and is looking forward to her next creative chapter doing art more than anything else.
- Devon, one of the generation of ground-breaking black actors in the seventies, who had to give it up to earn a living, now has enough financial, emotional and spiritual security to allow him to explore acting again. He was recently in a West End show and is shooting a part in a new feature film.
- From being unable to have time to herself to clear her house and start working on finding her own path, Jan changed her working days and manager. She enrolled on an art course, is fixing up her house and spending quality time with her children. She is preparing to go freelance and move to another country to be closer to her family.
- Alana has been cancer-free for several years. She recently left her job, went freelance and is planning a move to Portugal.
- Dalia kept taking care of her Inner Child, is planning her exit from her corporate job and is ready to ask for what she needs in her next role.
- Dancer and teacher Mia retrained as an interfaith minister to help more people. It's been a remarkable story from the unexpected changes and losses that Covid brought her.

- Bruce has a portfolio career, working as a tax expert and a coach, with time to work on his passion for music. His family and friends are now happy he made the changes he did.
- Pratam stopped saying yes to everything so he could develop his own creativity, and is now mentoring others to be creative, especially young men of colour like himself.
- Eva has built and leads a community platform for young women in business. She loves her new life, is doing what she believes in and is good at helping others.

I am excited to see what happens next for all of them. Their stories are not over. They are not different from you. They still struggle at times, and they still write their stories.

Exercise: Write It Down

Whether you tell your story to yourself or others, we all love a good narrative arc to engage us emotionally. Use these prompts to help you shape it – and write it down in your journal.

- Where did you start from?
- What was your initiation? What happened to bring you to the threshold of making a choice?
- What happened when you made that choice?
- What did you have to let go?
- What did you hold on to?

- What did you have to call forth from yourself and your resources?
- What obstacles arose?
- How did you feel?
- How you did you keep going?
- What gifts did you discover or receive?
- How were they helpful?
- What was your turning point?
- Where are you now?
- How is it different?
- How do you feel?
- What's possible for you now?

Always remember how far you have come. There will be days you'll spend on a plateau, feeling nothing has happened, or that your life has little meaning. On those days, read your story back again – you have been here before, and you will find a path.

A few years ago, I started a personal project I called 'Letters for Little Girls', initiated by the process of doing a very adult thing – writing a will. I don't have children of my own, but I have friends who do, and these children have had an important impact in my life. In fact, it was by being around two-year-old girls that I realized what it must have been like for me, at two years old, to lose my mother. As I was writing my will, I realized I wanted to leave something for them – just a small amount of money. But I didn't want them to use it for anything sensible like a smart outfit on their first day of work. I wanted them to use that money to have a small courageous adventure that would help them grow and find their own path. But how would they know to do that? I had to write them a letter. In this letter, I started to write how I had learned to grow and how much that gave to me and my life. Then one day, I found I couldn't write any more. I was stuck and lost. I realized that I had wandered the world, met interesting people and had remarkable experiences, but there was one place I had never been, because it was too hard. It was that small patch of earth in Ireland where my mother is buried. How could I write my letters advocating courage with integrity, when I didn't dare to venture there? I sat lost in the woods for quite some time before I decided to find a path to it, so I could write my own story as one of courage, and therefore write the letters that would inspire those little girls to be courageous too. That search became the living and writing of the story I have shared in this book.

So if it's hard to write your own story, picture someone you are writing it for, and write them a letter. It might be someone you know, perhaps your own children or relatives, perhaps it might be for someone you have never met but for whom you would like to wish an authentic, fulfilled and meaningful life. Have faith that in some way, how you chose to write your own life will be read by them as encouragement to live their own.

Endings and Beginnings

As I approach the end of this book, I want to slow down a little to savour it. Let's do this together at the place where you started, with the natural flow of the seasons. I invite you to pause and begin to notice how you feel right now, at the end of this book. As always, there's no right or wrong, nowhere you *should* be, just where you are now. Please journal and notice your own season at the end of this book.

Journal Questions

Spring. Perhaps you feel excited, ready to put what you have been learning into action.

Summer. Maybe you feel warmed up, already in your flow, through practising and learning as you went along.

Autumn. Perhaps you feel a little reflective, turning inwards, perhaps a little sad about letting go.

Winter. Maybe you feel the seeds of your next act are buried, ready for spring to bring them into life. For now, you feel patient and trusting.

Always remember, this is your story to write, and you already have the pen. Once you put down this book, your journey will continue. I salute your courage and whole-heartedness. It is my deepest wish that you live a life that has meaning for you. It's not really about quitting the day job and opening an award-winning craft beer microbrewery or even becoming a life coach. It's about being able to feel, at the end of your life, that you did your best, lived authentically and can now take your final rest, no matter what you believe may come next.

Appendix 1: Psychological–Spiritual Life Developmental Stages

Adapted from Erik Erikson's stages of psychosocial development and Bill Plotkin's wheel of eco-soulcentric stages of life.

- Early Childhood – ego formation: 'Is it okay to be me?', 'Can I trust the world?'
- Late Childhood – exploration: 'Is it okay for me to do things?'
- Early Adolescence – developing a social self: 'Can I make it in the world?'
- Late Adolescence – leaving home, independence: 'Who can I be?'
- Early (First) Adulthood – learning to be successful in the world: 'Can I create a life for myself?'
- Late (Second) Adulthood – developing mastery and living purpose: 'Can I be authentically me? Can I deliver my purpose to the world?'
- Early Elderhood – acceptance and community: 'Can I give to others?'
- Late Elderhood – wisdom and legacy: 'What have I left behind?'

Appendix 2: Signs of Burnout

Burnout is a state of physical and emotional exhaustion. It can occur when you experience long-term stress or when you have been in a physically or emotionally draining role in work or life for a long time. Here are some signs.

- Feeling as if you have to constantly prove your worth.
- Becoming a workaholic.
- Feeling tired and drained most of the time.
- Experiencing headaches, digestive issues or other illnesses.
- Finding it hard to concentrate.
- Intolerance, snappiness and aggression.
- Neglecting your needs and not being able to eat or sleep.
- Loss of motivation.
- Sense of inner emptiness, and attempting to fill this with work, food, sex, alcohol and drugs.
- Withdrawing from friends, family and partners.

We can confuse stress with burnout. Stress usually causes burnout, but burnout is not just stress. You may feel stressed because you have a tight deadline, a house move, or a relationship or parenting challenge. If these things happen often enough and you see no positive end to the situation you are in or no satisfaction in the work that you do and the life you live, you may be experiencing burnout. Not all of the factors of burnout are explicitly work-related. We face great pressures that are brought about by the demands of parenting, supporting elderly parents, isolation and worries about financial and job security and relationships, all of which are having a big impact on our wellbeing. Consider talking to a doctor or a mental health provider because these symptoms can also be related to health conditions, such as depression and anxiety.

Resources

Books

Ruth Allen, *Grounded: How Connection with Nature Can Improve Our Mental and Physical Wellbeing* (Welbeck, 2021).

William Bridges, *Transitions: Making Sense of Life's Changes*, 2nd edition (Da Capo, 2004).

James Hollis, *Living an Examined Life: Wisdom for the Second Half of the Journey* (Sounds True, 2018).

David Kelley and Tom Kelley, *Creative Confidence: Unleashing the Creative Potential Within Us All* (HarperCollins, 2015).

Peter Levine, *Healing Trauma: A Pioneering Program for Restoring the Wisdom of Your Body* (Sounds True, 2008).

Paul Linden, *Embodied Peacemaking: Body Awareness Education for Replacing Violence with Communion* (free download from www.being-in-movement.com).

Paul Linden, *It's All the Same – Except for the Differences: Body Awareness, Wholeness, Peace, Sustainability, 51 Years of Aikido Practice* (download available from www.being-in-movement.com).

Richard Louv, *The Nature Principle: Reconnecting with Life in a Virtual Age* (Algonquin, 2012).

Maitreyabandhu, *The Journey and the Guide: A Practical Course in Enlightenment* (Windhorse, 2015).

Kristen Neff, *Self-Compassion: The Proven Power of Being Kind to Yourself* (Yellow Kite Books, 2015).

Parker J. Palmer, *Let Your Life Speak: Listening for the Voice of Vocation* (John Wiley and Sons, 2000).

Bill Plotkin, *Nature and the Human Soul: Cultivating Wholeness and Community in a Fragmented World* (New World Library, 2008).

Rainer Maria Rilke, *Letters to a Young Poet*, translated by Charlie Louth (Penguin, 2012).

Richard Schwartz, *No Bad Parts: Healing Trauma and Restoring Wholeness with the Internal Family Systems Model* (Sounds True, 2021).

Hal and Sidra Stone, *Embracing Ourselves* (New World Library, 1998).

Bronnie Ware, *The Top Five Regrets of the Dying: A Life Transformed by the Dearly Departing*, 2nd edition (Hay House, 2019).

Irvin Yalom, *The Gift of Therapy: An Open Letter to a New Generation of Therapists and Their Patients*, revised edition (Piatkus, 2003).

Irvin Yalom, *Love's Executioner* (Penguin, 2013).

Websites, podcasts and apps

There are some great apps full of meditations, mindfulness practices, courses and more, including Insight Timer, Calm, Headspace and Meditation Oasis.

The London Buddhist Centre has great talks and meditations on YouTube.

Being Well with Dr Rick Hanson and Forrest Hanson – a podcast exploring the practical science of well-being.

Tara Brach's website and podcast includes meditations and talks: www.tarabrach.com.

Kristin Neff provides a wonderful resource with videos and exercises to help develop self-compassion at https://selfcompassion.org/.

Conversations with Annalisa Barbieri podcast – understand more about why you behave the way you do.
To learn more about emotional literacy, look up the emotions wheel online.

Organizations that offer support

Welldoing: www.welldoing.org. Find a therapist, counsellor or coach; this site also has lots of articles and resources.
British Association for Counselling and Psychotherapy: www.bacp.co.uk.
UK Council for Psychotherapy: www.psychotherapy.org.uk.
Life Coach Directory: www.lifecoach-directory.org.uk.

Acknowledgements

This book is based on the work I do with clients in the kitchen of coaching, so my first thanks are to all those who have worked with me in one-to-one sessions and in workshops, courses and talks. It takes courage and some sacrifices to commit to coaching or participate in a workshop or course. I feel deeply privileged that they trusted me. I learn every day from the people with whom I work, and they make me a better coach – and a better person as well.

Several clients agreed to the inclusion of their experiences in this book, along with others who have changed their lives and agreed to be interviewed and share their stories. All did so in order that their experiences might be useful to the readers of this book. I deeply appreciate their generosity and bravery.

Like all coaches, I stand on the shoulders of the teachers and wisdom-keepers of those who came before and taught me. I want to thank my teachers and the founders of the Co-Active Training Institute, Henry and Karen Kimsey-House, and Laura Whitworth, for the wonderful coach training I received. I also want to thank their teachers. I want to acknowledge and thank founder Mark Walsh and the teachers and community of the Embodied Facilitator Course, especially Paul Linden, who generously agreed to allow me to include his centering techniques. Thanks too to Carlos Glover and Sue Milner for all their wisdom and love of land, spirit and community, which supports me in many ways, not least through their Sacred Leadership Training. Finally, thanks to Mac Macartney, Tina Sharman, Stephan Pfaff, Joey Waterson, Fiona Barnes and all the incredible team at Embercombe, who created such a powerful environment for the Journey leadership retreat in September 2021. It was there that I made my commitment to write this book, spoke it aloud and was witnessed. All helped me give myself permission, and they are all examples of how we can all make a contribution to make the world a better place. Their trainings and teachings have greatly influenced the practices and ideas I bring into my own work, and into this book. If you are interested in learning more, then I heartily recommend you seek out and explore their work.

I have also had the pleasure and privilege of working with some wonderful organizations, creating and leading workshops and talks. As Head of Learning and a member of the faculty of The School of Life, I worked with thinkers, teachers and staff committed to helping people develop emotional skills. My thanks to Alain de Botton, Charlotte Neser, Caroline Brimmer, Will Brimmer, Raul Aparici, EJ Trivett, David Waters, Susan Kahn, Sarah Stein Lubrano, and many others. I have been honoured to work with a terrific team at Guardian Masterclasses, who have been hugely supportive of the workshops I have led for them, from which parts of this book have developed. Thank you Kirsty McCusker-Delicado, Brett Halsey, Omi Feeney and the rest of the team.

Along my own journey, I have received wonderful support and wisdom from other teachers, therapists and coaches who have helped me personally and also have influenced many of the exercises and insights in this book. Thanks to Liz Baron-Cohen, Kate Gauci, Rafael Boker, and the teachers at the London Buddhist Centre.

After completing my previous book on thoughtful leadership, I could feel in my heart that I wanted to create something for people facing change in their lives, but although the desire was there, a way to do it wasn't yet. So when I received a call from Emine Saner, who was writing an article for the *Guardian* on second acts in life, and looking for tips from a life coach, I was delighted. Little did I know what was going to happen next. Within a couple of days, Daniel Bunyard, Publishing Director at Penguin Michael Joseph, dropped me a line asking if I wanted a chat about the possibility of writing a book about it. With his encouragement, I spent a long weekend drafting a proposal, and that was the seed from which this book emerged.

Thanks to both Emine and Daniel, and to the terrific team at Penguin, who worked tirelessly and gave me so much encouragement and support, even when Covid didn't make it easy for them. My thanks especially to Fenella Bates, Agatha Russell, Paula Flanagan, Ella-Aliisa Kurki, Emma Horton, Stephanie Biddle and Olivia Thomas. Thanks also to my agent, Richard Pike at C+W, for being such a tower of support.

Writing is a lonely business. Ultimately this book is the story of a woman, a laptop and endless cups of tea. But I have not been alone. I have the support, kindness and wisdom of many dear friends. They haven't only supported me to write this book but to live a full life.

Deepest thanks to Rupert Davis, Maurits Kalff, Rachel Blackman, Francis Briers, Jess Tyrrell, Kelvin Omard, Dan Windsor, Daniel Vais, Mark Lipton, Yasmin Khan, Simon Confino, Lori Ramos, John Ashton, Anthea Barbary, Eliza Tyrrell, Janet Tyrrell, Jeffrey Stephens-Prince, Andrea White, Josette Bogerman, Jvan Morandi, Talula Sheppard, Jane Dancey, Dominic Leeds, Phil Askew, Samantha Clarke and Steve Savides. I also want to thank my birth relatives in Ireland and elsewhere, who accepted me with such kindness and thoughtfulness.

Finally, I want to thank my family. With my family, it's complicated, but it's very simple to me. I have two biological parents – Claire and Lionello – who loved me. I have two adoptive parents – Christine and Peter – and two brothers – Simon and Phillip – who love me. All are my family. I have not lacked their love, only, sometimes, an ability to receive it. I receive it all now, and my heart is fuller than I could have imagined possible.

Fiona Buckland is a life and leadership coach, speaker and writer, passionate about helping people develop deeper, wiser leadership of themselves and their lives.

A Fulbright scholar with a PhD in Performance Studies from New York University, the corporate clients she helps with purpose, connection and leadership span the world. She also facilitates Guardian Masterclasses, as well as running self-development courses. She is on the faculty of The School of Life, a global organisation devoted to teaching people how to live a more fulfilled life, where she was previously Head of Learning.

Her book, *Thoughtful Leadership: A Guide to Leading with Mind, Body & Soul* was published by Leaping Hare Press in 2021.

She lives between the sea and the hills in East Sussex. www.fionabucklandcoaching.com